Kenneth Lo is the foremost expert on Chinese cuisine writing and broadcasting in English. Born in Foochow, China, in 1913, he studied physics at Peking University and later English Literature at Cambridge and London. He has pursued a variety of careers during his time in Britain: as a diplomat, a fine-art publisher, an industrial relations and welfare officer for Chinese seamen, a journalist, a lecturer, and as a professional tennis player. He is best known, however, for his many authoritative books on Chinese cooking and eating. He has contributed articles and columns to innumerable journals and magazines, and has appeared many times on television. The Mayflower edition of his *Cooking the Chinese Way* has been successfully in print for twenty-five years. Now in his sixties, Kenneth Lo is still extremely active and productive, and this he attributes to the fact that he follows his own advice – about cooking and eating.

Also by Kenneth Lo

Kenneth Lo

Cooking the Chinese Way

MAYFLOWER
GRANADA PUBLISHING
London Toronto Sydney New York

Published by Granada Publishing Limited
in Mayflower Books 1969
Revised and reset 1972
Reprinted 1979

ISBN 0 583 19657 8

First published in Great Britain
by Arco Publications 1955
Copyright © Kenneth H C Lo 1955, 1963

Granada Publishing Limited
Frogmore, St Albans, Herts AL2 2NF
and
3 Upper James Street, London W1R 4BP
1221 Avenue of the Americas, New York, NY 10020, USA
117 York Street, Sydney, NSW 2000, Australia
100 Skyway Avenue, Toronto, Ontario, Canada M9W 3A6
110 Northpark Centre, 2193 Johannesburg, South Africa
CML Centre, Queen & Wyndham, Auckland 1, New Zealand

Made and printed in Great Britain by
C. Nicholls & Company Ltd
The Philips Park Press, Manchester
Set in Monotype Times

Granada Publishing ®

To my wife

*from whom I have learnt so much
of the kitchen, especially about
washing up afterwards!*

Contents

Chapter One

INTRODUCTION

What is the fatal charm of Chinese cooking, from which so many, once enamoured, have never recovered? What is its secret, which has caused an American culinary writer to exalt it as the greatest cooking in the world; and some Frenchmen to admit that it is more subtle than the French, which is always accepted and respected as the pre-eminent school in the West? Whether these verdicts or opinions are correct or not, it is certainly worthwhile to conduct a tour of inspection, if not as a connoisseur at least as a gastronomic tourist.

There is one thing of which there is no doubt; that is, during the last couple of decades, Chinese restaurants are establishing themselves and Chinese cooking is prospering in every capital and sizeable city in the world. This must be an attestation to the fact that the number of people in the West who are taking to Chinese food is on a rapid increase. That this rapid expansion should take place without the aid of organised capital or inspired organisation, but has gone forward in a purely haphazard, if not chaotic manner; and that in its expansion Chinese food has never feared any competition from any quarter, generally finding, in fact, most prosperity where the competition is keenest, is a pointer that there must be something intrinsically superior and vital in the goods preferred, in so far, in this case, as the welfare of our two decisive organs are concerned – the palate and the stomach.

If the cat is to be let at once out of the bag, the strength of Chinese cooking simply lies equally in its quality as well as its quantity: to get the right perspective, when thinking of the teeming dishes of China, one must imagine in terms of China's proverbial teeming millions (here to think of scores or hundreds is to indulge in the extreme of typical Sino-Saxon understatement); when considering the gastronomic poetry of some of its culinary products one should recall to mind the exquisite delicacy and harmony of Ming bowls, Sung vases and Tang horses. For after all, they are all part and parcel of the life and expression of the same people, and of the same heritage.

To become really "fatally charmed" by Chinese cooking one has to have some knowledge of certain ranges of its vast repertoire, as well as at least a nodding acquaintance with its first line top-dishes. One can no more pass a decisive opinion on Chinese cooking by a few visits to some Chinese restaurants in the West, than for an oriental fully to understand and appreciate the wonders and mysteries of western music by listening to a few bands of undistinguished pop.

Although, in this case, it would be wrong to counsel that "a little learning is a dangerous thing, drink deep or taste not the Pierian spring", remember that so much is cultivated taste, and one requires the palate of a connoisseur to fathom the fullest gastronomic meaning and significance; for every dish has its own gastronomic memories, which are blended with the particular personal memory of the individual dinner for the dish; and no dish can attain its full meaning unless both these memories co-exist. It is only through the co-existence of these strains of memories that the quality of the performance of a particular chef can become manifest –

his particular interpretation of the masterpiece. In this instance, much as it is in the case of music, the better one is acquainted with a composition, the more desirous one is to hear the performance and interpretation of a famous performer. In order, therefore, to qualify as a connoisseur and a judge, one must have not only the quantitative experience of the whole vast repertoire, but also a keen appreciation and qualitative experience of the historical background of the various interpretations of the compositions as one looks back through the steaming and aromatic corridor of one's own as well as a nation's gastronomic memories.

Still, that is to be a connoisseur and a judge, but much can be gleaned which is highly enjoyable and interesting as a tourist, and so long as one is aware of the topless pinnacles and enormous territories which lie beyond and behind, one is not likely to confuse the Pennines with the Himalaya. Besides, one never knows when one may become enamoured. Some, in fact many, have been known to fall at first taste, and when love is the guiding light and stomach the driving power, no pinnacle is too high, nor frontier too distant ("though it be ten thousand miles!") And love in the case of Chinese food is so catching and enchanting – surely to fall is a privilege, whether in youth or age?

To the uninitiated Westerner, Chinese cooking appears, like the "Chinese puzzle", something best left to the Chinese. To the initiated Westerner Chinese cooking has too much of the Himalayan appearance to invite serious tackling. However, the writer believes that this is only their superficial reaction. The challenge of the "Puzzle" (crossword or otherwise) and the challenge of the Himalaya are just the very types of challenge which no true-born Anglo-Saxon can let pass without throwing down his gauntlet. Who knows that one may not some day win the first prize, or cap the top of Everest? This book of one hundred recipes has been written to give some exercise and skirmishes in the foothills, and also to provide some beckoning from greater and more famous heights.

However, the more important reason why the writer would recommend Chinese cooking to the Westerner is that it is an extremely useful and practical asset to acquire. Complicated as it might at first appear, yet, like the Chinese language, it is in many ways comparatively simple. One does not have to stick to so many rules and regulations; one is, I think, allowed far more freedom than in comparative Western cooking. The point where a very strict and sometimes exalted standard is set is in the *art* of cooking, and not in the pseudo-science, such as in the strict measure of time and exactness of ingredients (Chinese cookery books only give discourse and advice, seldom details and precise measurements); and one has to develop for oneself a high sense of harmony in blending, the use of contrasts and surprises, and the right use of ingredients to enhance and bring out the natural flavour of a given food or to suppress its less agreeable but inherent tastes. It is because of this highly developed artistic sense of Chinese cooking that it is capable of its incalculable, innumerable variations, and, like the artist, who is able to produce any number of pictures and designs with a limited number of colours, so a Chinese chef can produce a large number of dishes out of a small range of materials. For this reason, we Chinese are generally less dependent on and tied down by what is given to us to work with than the English;

it is just because in Chinese cooking we can make something out of almost anything that it is such a useful and important art to acquire, especially for the hard-pressed housewife of today, or a bachelor who is not indifferent to the gnawing of his stomach.

Because so great a part of Chinese cooking is art and admits of so many interpretations, for *first-class* cooking inspiration is imperative. When you have inspiration – which means that in your mind you have a clear vision of exactly what you are aiming to do – you can be allowed a great deal of licence. Whilst, on the other hand, without inspiration, although you may be measuring your ingredients out spoonful by spoonful, and keeping your time with a stopwatch, your production may still be wide of the mark. The job of the chef in the kitchen is, therefore, precisely the same as that of the conductor of an orchestra, on a platform, and is often performed with the same flourish.

Since Chinese cooking admits of so much individual freedom, initiative and inventiveness, it must for all practical purposes be classified as a liberal art, and as such it can be taken up and indulged in by anybody, with more or less success and certain enjoyment. The proof of the pie is in the eating, and in this case we can only allow our palate and stomach to be the ultimate judge. For those whose nerves have been worn to shreds by the hectic strain of modern living, Chinese cooking can hold the fascination and relaxation of painting, over which it holds one distinct advantage, namely, you can eat the product of your efforts. For those who are artistically inclined, both the cooking and the eating will provide consuming pleasure.

As for raw materials and ingredients, it is a misconception that a great many exotic spices are used. In fact, in at least 80 per cent of Chinese cooking, all the raw materials can be obtained from any ordinary English market or provision shop. The essential thing is that the raw materials should be fresh and good. What few spices and ingredients are necessary or useful for the production of some Chinese dishes can all be obtained from oriental or Chinese provision shops, which now abound in London, or if one prefers one can always fall back on such well-known suppliers as Jackson or Fortnum and Mason of Piccadilly, where these days many brands of Chinese foods are prominently displayed. So should any reader feel sufficiently inclined to venture his hand for a trial in the gentle and liberal art of Chinese cooking, he would generally be able to assemble all the raw materials and ingredients he would require in a matter of a few short hours, or certainly in a couple of days. For my part I should sincerely like to wish him very good luck and good cooking! And experience tells that he will be richly rewarded.

Chapter Two

SOME FEATURES, INGREDIENTS AND PRINCIPLES OF CHINESE COOKING

Although in Chinese cooking we do use a number of sauces and spices which are unknown or not commonly used in the West, only the following two are basic: (1) Soya sauce; (2) Ve-tsin or Chinese gourmet powder (which can be substituted with a chicken stock-cube).

Oyster sauce, bean-curd cheese, fermented (semi-solid) red beans and black beans are essential only in more advanced and elaborate cooking.

If and when soya sauce is unobtainable, and there is no reason why this should be so, there is a very useful substitute called Vesop, which is produced in this country, and which is obtainable from any Continental or well-supplied provision shop. This sauce has in fact been found to be even better than soya sauce in Chinese cooking for flavouring soup and vegetables, but not so good in the frying and braising of meat.

Ve-tsin, or Chinese gourmet powder, is generally added in very small quantities to soups, stews, and gravies during the last minutes of their cooking. The powder has the unique quality of bringing out and enhancing the natural flavour of the food. Being a comparatively new introduction into Chinese cooking, it is looked upon askance by old master-chefs, who are suspicious of anything slightly chemical. But because of its helpful quality it has become a widely-used ingredient of Chinese culinary art (often too widely used!).

Basically, the methods used in Chinese cooking are the same as in Western cooking: namely, frying, stewing, braising, smoking, boiling, steaming, roasting. The difference is in the subtleties within each method.

Whilst in Western cooking meat is generally cooked whole, or in large pieces, as in the form of steaks or chops, in Chinese cooking meats are generally cooked in smaller pieces (about an inch or a couple of inches square), or they are diced into $\frac{1}{4}$ in. cubes, shredded into "ribbons", or cut into very thin slices, which makes them more amenable to the chopsticks, since the knife is never brought to the table, being considered a barbarous instrument. When meat is cooked whole in China, it is usually stewed or braised for such a length of time and to such tenderness, that it can be picked to pieces by a pair of chopsticks.

Because meat is often cooked in small pieces or slices, frying is much more widely used than in the West. Thus meat can generally be cooked by frying in one, two or three minutes. These are some half dozen words in Chinese which all denote frying: they range from rapid "explosive" frying, lasting under a minute, to frying followed by semi-braising, which may last up to a quarter of an hour. Because three-quarters of the frying done in China is shallow frying, where only a little oil is used, and only a very short time is required, it is a very economical form of cooking.

Chinese frying generally starts at a very leisurely pace, since all the ingredients require careful preparation and chopping up. It gradually works itself up to a crescendo, which is the actual frying, when the heat is usually turned up to its highest. When ingredients are added, one after another, the finale, with its grand stirring up, comes almost like one of Tchaikovsky's compositions when everything is thrown in.

In stewing and braising, as compared with Western cooking, Chinese cooking is interminable. You have the expression "cook to death". The idea is to cook beyond death! By the use of low fire and long cooking even the toughest meat or fowl could be reduced to the extremes of tenderness. (Here an asbestos mat is recommended). Adding to it the flavour of good quality soya sauce, and with Ve-tsin to bring out its natural flavour, we Chinese can afford to be optimistic even when confronted with some of the toughest propositions. Sometimes excellent dishes can be produced out of fairly hopeless materials.

One method or practice which is more widely used in Chinese cooking than Western cooking is the use of meat and vegetable to impregnate flavour into each other. This interpenetration of taste is extended widely to meat and fish, especially salted fish. The resultant taste is fit to kill. Cooked oysters, dried prawns, scallops, are often used; they add an inimitable taste in the frying of noodles and vegetables, and in the preparation of soup.

When a Chinese chef aspires towards greater heights his development is generally towards a more superb and perfect blending of taste, aroma and flavour, rather than towards a greater architectural elaboration, as seems to be the case in the West, judging from what one often witnesses at food competitions.

Recollecting all the more memorable dishes I have consumed during my two decades of unforgettable eating in China, it seems that the things which are generally striven for in Chinese cooking are:

(1) A certain crispness in tenderness in all things grilled

or fried (this applies also to vegetables) – "crispness" as contrasted to soft but somewhat messy tenderness.

(2) The retention or bringing out of the distinctive taste of each of the constituent ingredients of a dish, although they may find themselves in a considerable mixture.

(3) The searching for and bringing out of a unique or rare flavour, such as that of Shark's Fin, Birds' Nest, or a variety of fungi, through well-tuned cooking and a harmony supplied by the right preparation and choice of supplementary ingredients.

(4) A certain seasoned "drunken richness" in stews.

(5) A certain purity of taste and richness in flavour of all soups.

(6) A certain sweetness derived from freshness in the case of fish, and sweetness derived from purity in the case of vegetables.

(7) That crackling quality and a certain aromatic scent and flavour to be attained in all roasted, grilled, or dried-fried (using little sauce or dressing) fish, fowl or meat.

(8) Emphasis and enhancing of a given taste through contrast such as the taste of celery or ham, seasoned meat, salted fish, egg, bean-curd paste, against the comparative tastelessness of soft boiled rice.

(9) The attainment of balance in a dish by contrasting qualities of the ingredients – such as the use of pickled food to take away the excess of fat or richness.

(10) The use of certain ingredients to lend strength or a "bite" to a flavour otherwise of no distinction – such as the use of pickled fermented cabbage to fry with shredded pork; or fermented beans to fry or steam with fish.

(11) The achievement of beauty and richness in colour

– stews should either be deep brown or red; vegetables pure green or creamy white; fish pure white.

(12) The subtle eradication by the use of certain ingredients such as ginger, garlic, onions and wine, of all inherent flavours or smells which are not wholly agreeable.

Chapter Three

COOKING OF RICE

In China rice is served in three basic forms:

(a) Soft rice or Congee, which is used at breakfast time, is in effect a watery rice gruel, generally eaten with salted or strong-flavoured food, such as salted egg, salted turnips, preserved "ancient egg", peanut fried in salt, ham, fried salted fish, Chinese "cheese" made from soya bean curd, which has an extraordinary captivating flavour when, or if, one gets used to it. It is presumed that at breakfast time one's mouth and palate are still so thick that they require something strong or salty to jolt them into sensibility and awakeness (hence probably the popularity here of bacon and kipper for breakfast).

On the other hand, the thin wateriness of "Congee" helps to give the mouth a refreshing "wash-down" effect; in fact, it provides almost a taste of sweetness after the strong-flavoured or salty food. Hence the popularity of Congee in China, not only in the South where it is universally used, but also in the North, where steamed bread or dumpling is the order of the day – used in all three meals – but is served with Congee at breakfast time.

Congee is produced by simply boiling rice in varying quantities of water for about an hour to one and a half hours. Generally four to eight times as much water as rice is used, but the proportion of water to rice really depends upon the final dilution one requires.

(b) The second way in which rice is commonly served is the usual plain steamed rice, which is served both during lunch and dinner. Although it is as often prepared by boiling as steaming, if the former method is used, being the simpler of the two, since not everyone possesses an adequate steamer, one has to be extremely careful during the last ten minutes of the cooking not to burn the rice: during this last stage of cooking, the heat should be turned very low, and preferably an asbestos mat should be inserted, so that the rice would, in effect, be steamed in its own moisture.

In preparing rice in this manner, one would generally employ about two and a half times as much water as rice. After having washed the rice, place it in a saucepan and pour in the water. Bring it to the boil, keeping the lid securely closed, and leave it to simmer for about six to seven minutes, or until the rice is no longer watery. Now lower the heat to the minimum and insert the asbestos sheet. Leave the pan to simmer for a further ten to twelve minutes. The rice will now be ready to serve. Each grain will be soft but dry.

The established way of cooking this type of rice in China is to steam it in a bamboo basket-steamer, which is placed over a pan of boiling water. Rice prepared in this manner is the staple food of China. In the areas north of the Yangtse River where steamed bread or dumpling (called Mun Tao) is also the staple food, rice is often served in conjunction with it, at least in all the better-fed families.

Although Chinese are rice-eaters, it is a misconception to believe, as many Westerners do, that the Chinese people eat nothing but rice. Certainly rice is our staple food and forms the main bulk of each meal, but a number of tasty dishes are usually served with it. An average meal will consist of one or two soups – a vegetable soup and a meat soup – a meat dish, an egg or fish dish, and one or two vegetable dishes served in conjunction with rice. In wealthier families where more than half a dozen dishes are served during each meal, rice merely acts as a "buffer" to all the rich and tasty dishes, which are placed on the table all together in buffet fashion. During banquets or formal parties, no rice is served at all (since there is such an abundance of other types of food), and the dishes – as a rule numbering about one dozen or more – are brought in at ten-minute intervals, and served and consumed course after course.

(c) The third way in which rice is prepared and served in China is the semi-solid or "porridgy" rice, which is made either from steamed rice boiled up with the addition of extra water, or congee thickened with the use of a greater proportion of rice in the boiling. As this form of rice requires less of the grain to cook than steam rice and is more sustaining than congee, it is usually served in the poorer families. For those in greater poverty in the south, rice in this form is often boiled up with shredded dried sweet potato, which gives it further bulk. In the north the bulk is made up of steamed dumpling (a very filling food) and large flour "big cakes" (like crumpets, but drier and about four times their size) eaten with a lot of garlic.

Apart from these three basic forms in which rice is served in China – here rice more or less takes the place of bread and potatoes in Western meals – all the other fancy forms of rice should be classified as snacks or desserts. They bear much the same relation to the three staple forms of rice as sandwich to bread or potato crisp to plain boiled potato. However, as some of them are quite popular and well known even in the West, and they would probably be more easily found under the classification of rice rather than snacks and desserts, the recipes for several of them are given here:

1. FRIED RICE

Although this dish is often and proudly served in European Chinese restaurants, it is never considered a highly presentable dish in China. By that I mean it is not something one would find on the menu of a reputable Chinese restaurant, nor a dish which a proud housewife would wish to place on her table when entertaining any except the most familiar acquaintances. For this dish is in its nature ranked more or less as scrambled eggs on the English menu.

Nevertheless, as a dish it is capable of far greater variations and interpretations than scrambled eggs, and when cooked with the best ingredients can be most appetising. Being a snack rather than a course or a dish, it is generally eaten on its own rather than served with numerous other dishes at meal-time; but it is generally eaten with a simple soup.

The most common form of fried rice is the egg and ham, or the egg and meat fried rice, fried with onions, and perhaps with shrimps and mushrooms thrown in for added taste and de luxe effect.

1 large plateful of cold steam rice
2 or 3 fresh eggs
¼ lb. ham or cooked meat
2 medium-sized onions
2 tbsp. lard

Cut the onions into small diced pieces and fry in lard in a large frying pan over a fierce heat for one minute. Add the rice and break up all the lumpy pieces. Fry until the rice is slightly brown. Pour in the two or three beaten eggs, turn and toss the rice quickly so that the frying and heat are even all over the pan. Add shredded ham, continue to stir and turn for a further two minutes. Add salt or soya sauce (about one and a half tablespoons) to taste. If such things as shrimps and mushrooms are to be added, they should be put in at the same time as the ham.

Properly cooked fried rice is a dry (it must never be messy) aromatic dish, hence it should be served concurrently with at least one soup.

2. SOFT RICE (CONGEE) WITH ASSORTED INGREDIENTS

1 breakfast cup of rice
   (glutinous type if available)
2 oz. dried scallops
2 oz. dried shrimps
2 oz. ham
2 oz. cooked chicken meat
1 tbsp. lard
1 tsp. salt
2 tbsp. Vesop or soya sauce

Prepare the rice by boiling in six cups of water for ½ hour. Meanwhile prepare the ingredients by soaking the shrimps (after removing tails and heads) and scallops in Vesop. Add the mixture, with lard, into the boiling rice, together with sliced chicken meat or ham or both, and simmer over a low heat for another ½ hour. Season with salt and pepper and serve.

3. CHICKEN SOFT-RICE

1 spring chicken
2 or 3 slices ginger
4 spring onions (chopped)
1 tbsp. salt
6 tbsp. soya sauce
1 large onion

Dress and clean the chicken and boil it in a pan with six to seven cups of water over a low heat with ginger and onion (sliced) for one hour. Add salt and boil for another $\frac{1}{2}$ hour. Remove the chicken now from the pan and cut it into $1\frac{1}{2}$ in. pieces.

Meanwhile, wash the rice (use glutinous rice if available) and boil it in the chicken soup for thirty-five minutes, or until it becomes a soft uniform mess. At this point divide the cut chicken into six or so serving bowls, into each of which has been placed 1 tbsp. soya sauce and some chopped spring onion. Pour the soft rice into each of the bowls, and serve after seasoning with a little pepper.

This dish is considered a dainty snack in China and is favoured by society ladies and mistresses, wealthy but corruptible would-be mandarins and merchants. In the West it is highly to be recommended for exhausted business executives with suspicion of duodenal ulcers.

4. THE "EIGHT-TREASURE" RICE

This is the only Chinese rice dish which comes anywhere near to the English conception of a dessert or pudding. This is nothing like the traditional rice pudding of the West, but approaches more nearly in shape and form, the Christmas pudding.

1 lb. glutinous rice
6 tbsp. ground suet
5 tbsp. sugar
2 tbsp. barley
6 tbsp. honeyed dates
4 tbsp. candied cherries
4 tbsp. lotus seeds
4 tbsp. dragon eyes
6 prunes
4 tbsp. candied orange peel
4 tbsp. any green candied fruit
4 tbsp. almonds
2 tbsp. lard
   (for anything that is not available
   substitute with raisins and walnuts)

Boil glutinous rice in four cups of water until fairly dry. Mix in suet and sugar and carry on over a very low heat (insert asbestos mat) for a further five minutes.

Meanwhile blanch the lotus seeds and nuts, and cut the fruit into even sizes and slice candied fruits into strips. Now use a large pudding basin and oil the inside over with lard and then cover with a one-third-inch layer of glutinous rice. Arrange the fruits and coloured candied fruits in attractive designs on the layer of rice, and press them through to the surface so that they will show when the pudding is later turned out on a plate. Build the contents up in the basin in this same manner, layer after layer alternately of coloured fruit and rice, until it is full. Place the basin in a steamer and steam for forty minutes. Turn the pudding onto a hot plate when ready to serve.

"Eight-treasure" rice is considered a festive dish in

China. It can be recommended to Western housewives to try as an alternative to, or as an additional, Christmas pudding.

Chapter Four

NOODLES

We have come next to noodles, because, after rice and steamed bread (or dumplings), they are the next staple food of China. Chinese noodles vary in thickness from the thickest Italian spaghetti to the finest vermicelli. They are all made from dough, which is constituted of wheat or rice flour (mainly wheat flour), or pea starch, mixed with varying quantities of egg and water. But the distinguishing character of Chinese noodles lies not in their constitution, but in the methods of cooking them.

There are four main ways in which Chinese noodles are served:
- (a) Noodles prepared with sauce (generally a sauce made from bean-paste).
- (b) Noodles served in gravy.
- (c) Noodles in soup.
- (d) Fried noodles.

Under these four major categories, Chinese noodles, having few taboos or limitations as to the ingredients with which they can be mixed, can be cooked, blended and served in several hundred different ways.

Fried noodles and noodles in soup and gravy are generally served as a snack at tea time or at supper time late at night. The ingredients most frequently used in conjunction with noodles are shredded meat, chicken meat, ham, shrimps, prawns, lobster, oysters and eggs, together with any form of vegetables, mushrooms or fungi, which might be available.

For a light tea time snack, as an appetiser to precede an evening of banqueting, on the occasion of a wedding, grand birthday anniversary, funeral, reception or memmorial get-together, a light egg-noodle is generally served in a very clear chicken soup garnished with a few strands of shredded ham.

With noodles which are served at ordinary tea time to satisfy a possible appetite far more substantial ingredients are used.

In fried noodles the ingredients, which may consist of meat and prawns together with a number of vegetables, such as mushrooms "wood-ears" (a kind of fungi), celery, shredded carrots, are generally cooked independently of the noodles, and are fried together only at the last moment.

A very attractive and tasty way of cooking noodles is to cook them in the gravy of the ingredients which have been prepared separately. This gravy is often thickened with the addition of a little cornflour. In the final stage of the preparation the noodles and ingredients are cooked together for a few minutes which enables the gravy to impregnate the noodles with its generally very tasty flavour.

The favourite "Birthday Noodle" is distinguished by the addition to the usual noodles in gravy of a hard-boiled egg, which has been dyed or painted red.

By far the tastiest of all noodles are noodles fried or stewed with oysters. In such a preparation oysters are seldom used alone; they are generally used in conjunction with meat and a variety of fungi. Here the interpenetration of taste is brought to such an effective point that it has an utterly devastating effect on all those who are fond of highly tasty food and inclined to the swallowing of long noodle-like preparations. Its immense value lies in its ability to satisfy and entertain the aged and elderly, who can no longer enjoy the rough and tumble of life and do not possess sufficient teeth to indulge themselves in chewing steaks and chops.

In the North, where noodles are served as one of the staple foods – these are generally larger calibre noodles which resemble the Italian spaghetti – they are, as a rule, eaten with a sauce which has its base in soya bean paste (here minced meat can be added). This preparation, which is served at a regular meal, is a very economical dish, as both large noodles and fermented soya paste are comparatively inexpensive. Yet a dish consisting of these two ingredients, plus a little garlic, minced meat and raw spring onion, can be so appetising and easy to swallow in quantity that the diner is often unaware of the amount he has eaten until he has to struggle to rise from his seat.

A favourite noodle dish of the South is the rice-flour noodle. This is generally whiter in appearance than the wheat-flour noodle. In Fukien and Kwangtung, the two southern provinces, they are often cooked with fresh oysters, dried mussels, together with spring onion, sliced pork, "wood-ear", mushrooms, dried lily flowers as supplementary ingredients, either in the form of stewed or fried noodles.

Pea-starch noodles, which are completely transparent, are usually reserved for use in soup, or for the preparation and cooking of stewed and fried vegetables. Possibly because of their round slippery shape, and partly because they are able to carry a lot of tasty gravy with them, they have an amazing "ball-bearing" effect in their ability to help the swallowing of quantities of rice. Invariably when a well-prepared dish of this kind appears on the table, the diners find it difficult to rise after the meal.

Indeed, here I must mention that one of the greatest drawbacks and disadvantages of Chinese food is simply that, if it is well-prepared one is inclined to tuck away so much unawares that one invariably over-eats. This may be attributable to the fact that when one eats in the buffet style and is not limited to the food placed immediately in front, on one's own plate, one invariably develops a knack of gathering all the choicest bits from all the choicest dishes in the most unobtrusive and inconspicuous manner and causing them to disappear, without occasioning the least embarrassment anywhere, except where it matters the longest – in one's stomach.

1. THE NORTHERN SOYA PASTE NOODLE

1 lb. noodles (largest calibre)
4 tbsp. soya paste
½ lb. minced pork
10 spring onions
6 radishes
1 tsp. chopped ginger
1 small cucumber
3 tbsp. lard
½ lb. pea sprouts

Mix the minced pork, chopped ginger, ½ chopped onion and smashed garlic together and fry with 2 tbsp. of oil in a large frying pan for four or five minutes. Add the soya bean paste and, while stirring, add one cup of water slowly. Stir the mixture for a further ten minutes and the sauce is ready.

Now chop the remainder of the onions fine, slice the cucumber into thin strips, peel and slice the radishes lengthwise, and immerse the pea sprouts for three minutes in boiling water and drain. These ingredients are not to be cooked but are to be put into separate dishes on the dining table as an accompaniment to the noodles.

Meanwhile, the noodles should be prepared in the usual, way, which is to put them in boiling water and cook for fifteen minutes (use a fork to separate them while boiling). Chinese noodles take a shorter time to cook than Italian spaghetti. Remove from pan, drain. Divide them into equal portions and place them in separate bowls for each individual diner.

Each person at the table helps himself to a tablespoon or two of the soya paste sauce and the other ingredients from the various bowls, which he mixes well with his noodles before eating.

The enjoyment of this type of noodles is very much a cultivated taste; it is particularly indigenous to the Good Earth, especially the Great Northern Plain, of China.

2. STANDARD FRIED NOODLES

$\frac{1}{2}$ lb. noodles
$\frac{1}{4}$ lb. sliced pork
   (in strips)
$\frac{1}{4}$ lb. shrimps
$\frac{1}{4}$ lb. cabbage
$\frac{1}{4}$ lb. bamboo shoots
3 or 4 mushrooms
$\frac{1}{2}$ tbsp. cornflour
2 slices ginger
2 tbsp. soya sauce

1 tsp. salt
3½ tbsp. lard
½ tsp. sesame oil

Cut the cabbage and bamboo shoots into 1½ in. length
strips. Soak the mushrooms in hot water for ten minutes
and also cut into slices. Fry the sliced pork, bamboo
shoots and cabbage in 2 tbsp. of lard, adding salt, for
six to seven minutes, and remove from heat.

Mix 1½ tbsp. soya sauce, ginger, sherry, shelled shrimps
and cornflour. Fry the mixture in ½ tbsp. of lard for three
minutes. Now mix in the already fried pork, bamboo
shoots and cabbage. Fry a further one and a half minutes.

Now place the remainder of the lard in the frying pan
and pour in the boiled noodles, after draining. Add
remainder of soya sauce, salt and sesame oil and stir
and turn for five minutes. Now add the cooked pork,
shrimps, cabbage, etc., and stir over a fierce heat for two
minutes and serve.

3. STEWED NOODLES IN GRAVY

½ lb. noodles
¼ lb. pork
1 cup chicken broth
1 small cauliflower
4 medium size mushrooms
½ tbsp. sesame oil
1 oz. "wood-ear" (fungi)
2 spring onions
½ tbsp. cornflour
½ tbsp. soya sauce
¼ tsp. Ve-tsin (gourmet powder or 1 stock-cube)
¼ tbsp. lard or vegetable oil

Prepare the noodles in the usual way, by boiling in two pints of water for twelve minutes. Drain and pass through cold water under a tap.

Slice the pork against grain into $1\frac{1}{2}$ in. strips. Chop the cauliflower into $\frac{1}{2}$ in. sq. pieces. Fry them together in oil for four minutes together with sliced mushroom with a pinch of salt. Now add chopped (about $\frac{1}{2}$ in. length) spring onion, wood-ear, and soya sauce, and fry for a further two minutes before adding chicken broth into which cornflour had been mixed. Stir stew for a further ten minutes.

Meanwhile, fry the cooked noodles in the seasme oil for two minutes. Pour the pork, mushroom, cauliflower mixture over the noodles, together with gravy, add the gourmet powder (or crushed stock-cube,) and leave to simmer for three minutes over a low heat before serving.

4. CHICKEN-HAM NOODLES IN CHICKEN BROTH

(This is the noodle of occasion, served at weddings, funerals, etc.).

1 lb. of thin egg noodles
$\frac{1}{4}$ lb. cooked chicken meat
$\frac{1}{4}$ lb. smoked ham
2 pints of chicken broth
2 spring onions
1 tsp. chopped ginger
1 tsp. salt
$\frac{1}{2}$ tsp. Ve-tsin (gourmet powder, or 1 stock-cube)

Prepare the noodles as usual by boiling and rinsing with cold water; divide into eight equal portions and place them in eight separate bowls.

Boil the chicken meat and ham in the chicken broth for fifteen minutes. Remove from broth and slice into strips about 2 in. long. Now add to the broth salt, chopped ginger, spring onion, and gourmet powder. Bring to boil once more. Pour the broth immediately in equal portions into the eight bowls, which should be kept hot, garnish with strips of chicken meat and ham and serve.

5. SOUP NOODLES WITH CHICKEN, HAM AND OYSTERS

1 lb. noodles
¼ lb. chicken meat
2 oz. smoked ham
12 medium size oysters
2 pints chicken broth
1 oz. "wood-ear"
1 tbsp. lard
2 young leeks
2 spring onions
¼ tsp. chopped ginger
6 mushrooms
2 tbsp. sherry
1 tbsp. soya sauce
1 tsp. salt

Slice the ham into 1½ in. strips and boil in chicken broth for five minutes. Remove oysters from shells and add them to the broth. Add salt and chopped ginger, simmer for ten minutes. Add noodles and onions and simmer for a further two to three minutes.

Fry sliced chicken meat, with sliced mushrooms and

wood-ear (after softening the latter by soaking in hot water) and sliced leeks, for five minutes, in soya sauce and lard. Lace with sherry and pour the mixture over the noodles and serve. If you like shellfish this is one of the tastiest dishes in creation, wonderful on a cold winter's day.

6. VEGETARIAN FRIED NOODLES

1 lb. noodles
¼ lb. bamboo shoots
8 mushrooms
4 oz. spinach
4 oz. Chinese fermented pickled vegetable
  (Tsa Tsai)
5 tbsp. vegetable oil
1 tsp. salt
2 tbsp. soya sauce
½ tbsp. cornflour
½ tsp. Ve-tsin (gourmet powder, or 1 stock-cube)
2 tbsp. sherry

Slice the bamboo shoots into 1½ in. strips, wash the spinach, wash the mushrooms and soak in a cup of boiling water; slice the pickled vegetable into 2 in. strips.

Fry the bamboo shoots in oil for two minutes; add spinach, mushroom, pickled vegetable, with a pinch of salt, and continue to fry for three minutes. Now add the pre-cooked noodles and stir for two minutes, mixing thoroughly. Mix the cornflour with the mushroom water and soya sauce and pour the mixture onto the noodles.

Mix well, add Ve-tsin and bring to boil. Lace with sherry, pepper, and serve immediately.

The fermented pickled vegetable brings out a tastiness which no ordinary vegetable can provide.

Chapter Five

CHINESE SOUPS

The ordinary Chinese soup is made from the same base as Western soup: bone stock (chicken or pork bone). But the superior type of Chinese soup is made of broth distilled from chicken and pork, with not more than fifteen per cent ham and beef added to enhance taste. To produce a given quantity of soup you require the same quantity in weight of meat (in the proportion of five of chicken, seven of lean pork, one each of ham and beef). You start off with one hundred per cent more water, after the first boiling and skimming, you continue to simmer for three or four hours over a very low heat, until the quantity of water becomes reduced to about the same quantity as the weight of meat. This is as you can imagine a very concentrated as well as a very expensive broth, and is practicable to prepare only on a large scale, such as in restaurants. When preparing, so long as no violent boiling is allowed, the broth can always be kept clear; and Chinese soups are as a rule clear soups.

On the other hand, quite a number of Chinese soups can simply be made from tap water, and prepared in next to no time, and yet they can possess attractive and satisfying taste (several of the soups given below are of this variety) as well as a very presentable appearance.

Because Chinese food is eaten in the buffet style, soup is drunk not at the beginning of the meal, but between mouthfuls of a variety of food. For this reason it has quite a different function from Western soup, and probably serves a more useful purpose, both at the moment when they are imbibed and when further afield in the digestive tracts, since it is probably helpful to digestion for every couple of mouthfuls of food to be chased down by a mouthful of soup; and especially when rich meat dishes are generally accompanied by fresh vegetable soups, and plain vegetarian food is accompanied and enriched by meat broth.

Since a good-class Chinese meal would consist of certainly more than half-a-dozen dishes (often about ten) the number of varieties of soups served are not limited to one as in the West, but may run up to two or more. Indeed, the people of my home province of Fukien are so fond of soup that one of my Cantonese friends was considerably surprised when he sat down to dinner with a Fukienese family and found that of the ten dishes served seven were soups or semi-soups!

1. EGG-FLOWER SOUP

2 *pints of bone stock*
  (*or tap water*)
2 *fresh eggs*
2 *spring onions* (*chopped*)
1 *tsp. vinegar*
2 *tbsp. soya sauce*
  (*or preferably Vesop*)
½ *tsp. Ve-tsin* (*gourmet powder or 1 stock-cube*)
1 *tsp. salt*
½ *tsp. lard*
Pinch of pepper

Bring bone stock (or water) to boil. Remove from fire. Pour beaten egg, mixed with a little oil, slowly into the stock in the thinnest stream. Add chopped spring onions and salt. Bring to boil again. Add Vesop, Ve-tsin, vinegar, pepper. Stir with ladle, and soup is ready to serve.

This is one of the most commonly served soups in Chinese homes and should not take more than ten minutes to prepare. Although extremely simple, it is quite tasty. The vinegar gives it that extra bite, which also enables it to wash away any excessive richness in other dishes. The addition of sliced mushroom to enhance interest is quite permissible.

2. SLICED PORK AND WATERCRESS SOUP

2 pints bone stock
4 oz. lean pork
4 oz. watercress
2 spring onions
2 tsp. cornflour
2 tbsp. soya sauce or Vesop
½ tsp. Ve-tsin (gourmet powder or 1 stock-cube)
1 tsp. salt
Pinch of pepper

Slice pork into ½ in. pieces and mix with a cornflour paste (cornflour mixed with tbsp. water). Bring two pints of stock (or water) to boil, add salt and pork and simmer for five to six minutes. Add watercress and chopped onions, as well as Vesop and Ve-tsin. Boil gently for further five minutes. Pepper and serve.

3. PORK PELLET AND MUSHROOM SOUP

Carry on with the same ingredients as above, except for substituting mushrooms (six or eight) for watercress. Button mushrooms are preferable in this case, as they don't darken the soup as much as the larger types. If larger ones are used they should be washed and soaked before using.

4. MEATBALL AND CHINESE TRANSPARENT VERMICELLI SOUP

2 pints bone stock
6 oz. minced pork
2 oz. Chinese pea-starch noodles
2 spring onions
1 tbsp. lard
1 tsp. salt
2 tbsp. soya sauce (or Vesop)
½ tsp. Ve-tsin (gourmet powder or 1 stock-cube)

Make meat balls about the size of pigeons' eggs by mixing minced meat with cornflour paste, with the addition of a pinch of salt and pepper. Fry in oil for three to four minutes until quite brown, and remove and drain. Chop spring onions into ¼ in. lengths, wash vermicelli in hot water. After draining, put it in a pan of boiling stock and boil for three minutes. Add the meat balls and continue to boil for five minutes. Now add the spring onions and the seasoning. Simmer for a further three minutes and the soup is ready to serve.

5. CHICKEN-NOODLE-HAM AND BAMBOO SHOOT SOUP

2 pints chicken bone broth
3 oz. chicken meat
3 oz. egg noodle
2 oz. bamboo shoots
2 oz. ham
1 tsp. salt
1 tbsp. Vesop
1 tbsp. sherry
Pepper

Slice chicken meat, bamboo shoots and ham into 1½ in. match-stick strips. Simmer the bamboo shoots and chicken meat in two pints of stock for ten minutes. Add noodle and salt and continue to simmer for a further five minutes. Add all the seasonings. Distribute the sliced ham evenly over the soup. Boil gently for a further minute and serve.

6. CHICKEN-HAM-AWABI-BAMBOO SHOOT SOUP

3 oz. chicken meat
3 oz. awabi (tinned or dried)
2 oz. ham
3 oz. bamboo shoots
2 slices ginger
1 tbsp. Vesop
1 tbsp. sherry
1 tsp. salt
Pepper

Cut chicken and awabi into thin slices. Simmer in chicken bone stock together with sliced ginger, bamboo shoots, which have been cut into match-stick strips, for fifteen minutes. Sprinkle sliced ham over the soup. Add all the seasonings and boil gently for a further two minutes and serve.

7. CHICKEN-HAM-AND-MUSHROOM SOUP

2 pints chicken bone stock
3 oz. chicken meat
6–8 mushrooms (Chinese dried mushrooms if available)
3 oz. ham
1 tsp. salt   1 tbsp. sherry
1 tbsp. Vesop   ½ tsp. Ve-tsin (1 chicken stock cube)
Pepper

Cut the mushrooms into quarters after soaking in a cup of boiling water for half an hour. Boil shredded ham gently in chicken bone stock for ten minutes. Add the mushrooms and mushroom water to the pan. Add sliced chicken meat and continue to simmer for ten minutes. Now add the seasonings (sherry and Gourmet powder), pepper to taste. Sprinkle the shredded ham over the soup, and serve.

8. CHICKEN-AND-HAM FISH SOUP

½ lb. fish (halibut, bass, sole, skate)
2 pints chicken bone stock
2 oz. ham
1 tbsp. cornflour
1 tsp. salt

    3 spring onions (chopped)
    2 slices ginger
    2 tbsp. Vesop
    1 tbsp. sherry
    ½ tbsp. vinegar
    ½ tsp. Ve-tsin (1 chicken stock cube)

Cut the fish into ½ in. pieces. Mix with cornflour paste. Boil the fish gently in chicken stock for five minutes. Add sliced ham, and continue to simmer for five minutes. Now add all the seasonings, sprinkle the chopped onions over the soup, and serve.

9. "ONE TUN" OR CHINESE RAVIOLI SOUP

    2 pints pork or chicken bone stock
    2 spring onions (chopped)
    6 oz. Chinese ravioli
    1 tsp. salt
    1 tbsp. soya sauce or Vesop
    ½ tsp. Ve-tsin (or gourmet powder)

Chinese ravioli or *One Tun* is made by placing finely minced pork, mixed with chopped onion, a small quantity of garlic soya sauce, and cornflour, in between two very thin sheets of dough (about 1½ in. sq.). The meat content is sealed inside by pressing down the edge of the dough with a knife or fork. Or, alternatively, the meat content can be folded in a slightly larger sheet (about 2½ in. sq.) of dough and sealed inside by folding over and pressing the edges together.

    Gently boil the chopped spring onions in chicken stock for five minutes, add all the seasoning and some pepper to taste. Fry the ravioli in deep fat until they are distinctly crispy on the outside. Remove the ravioli from pan and drain thoroughly. Pour the soup into a large Chinese soup bowl (or into as many soup plates as required). Add the ravioli into the soup immediately before serving. Thus the ravioli will float on top and the diner will find it still in a cracking state in his mouth while he is drinking soup: a pleasant sensation.

An easier and more leisurely way of preparing this soup is simply to simmer the pieces of ravioli in the stock together with chopped onion for about ten minutes before adding all the seasoning and serving. Some people prefer it prepared this way. The taste of dough cooked in stock has a special, endearing appeal to the connoisseurs of noodle soups.

10. BIRD'S (SEA SWALLOW) NEST SOUP

3 oz. dried bird's nest (a dried gelatinous substance)
3 oz. white chicken meat
3 egg whites
1 oz. ham (chopped)
1 pint chicken broth
1 pint ham broth
1 tbsp. sherry
½ tbsp. cornflour
1 tsp. salt

Soak bird's nest in boiling water and leave to stand for five to six hours. Drain and remove any stray feather which may still remain with tweezers. Add sherry and a cupful of hot water to the now gelatinous bird's nest.

Place the mixture in a small saucepan and simmer very gently for half an hour.

Mince the chicken meat very fine, mix with egg white and beat them up together.

Meanwhile add the chicken and ham broth to the pan containing the bird's nest. Bring to boil and leave to simmer gently for fifteen minutes. Now stir the mixture of minced chicken and egg white into the bird's nest in chicken-and-ham broth, in a fine steady stream. Add corn-flour to thicken whilst stirring continually. Leave to simmer gently for ten minutes before garnishing with chopped ham and serve in a large bowl.

11. CRAB AND VINEGAR SOUP

   1 large crab
   2 pints chicken bone stock
   2 spring onions (*chopped*)
   2 eggs
   2 tomatoes
   2 tbsp. sherry
   2 tbsp. Vesop
   2 tbsp. vinegar
   1 tsp. salt
   1 tsp. chopped ginger
   ½ tsp. Ve-tsin (*1 chicken stock cube*)

If the crab is raw steam it for half an hour. Scrape out all the meat, including its eggs onto a dish. Fry the crab-meat in oil with salt, chopped ginger and sliced tomato for five minutes. Remove from heat and slowly pour in beaten egg in a fine stream. Stir and bring to boil again, and add all the seasoning and continue to boil gently for five minutes. Sprinkle with the chopped spring onions, and serve.

12. FISHBALL SOUP

½ lb. raw fish (*Halibut, turbot, whiting, sole, haddock, etc.*)
2 oz. lean pork
1 tbsp. cornflour
2 pints chicken stock
1 egg white
1 tsp. salt
2 tbsp. Vesop
2 tbsp. sherry
1 tbsp. vinegar
2 spring onions
½ tsp. Ve-tsin (*1 chicken stock cube*)
Pepper

Chop or mince the raw fish and mix it thoroughly with egg white and minced pork. Add cornflour and one tbsp. of water. Beat the mixture up until it becomes a light homogeneous paste. Make the balls of about the size of pigeon eggs with the paste.

Boil the fish paste balls in chicken broth for ten minutes. Add the chopped spring onions and seasonings and serve after simmering for another five minutes.

13. HAM AND SPRING GREEN SOUP

2 pints pork bone stock
6 oz. spring greens
4 oz. ham

2 oz. bamboo shoots
2 oz. pea-starch noodles
1 tsp. salt
2 tbsp. soya sauce or Vesop
½ tsp. Ve-tsin (1 chicken stock-cube)
Pepper

Wash the spring greens thoroughly, cut into 1 in. wide slices, and soak in a large bowlful of water for three-quarters of an hour. Slice ham and bamboo shoots into match-stick strips. Bring chicken stock to boil in a saucepan. Add ham, bamboo shoots, and vermicelli, and simmer for fifteen minutes. Now add the spring greens, stock-cube, the seasonings, boil gently for ten more minutes and serve.

14. BEEF AND TURNIP SOUP

1 lb. lean beef
3 medium turnips
3 pieces sliced ginger
1 tsp. salt
2 tbsp. soya sauce or Vesop
½ tsp. Ve-tsin (1 stock-cube)
Pepper

Cut the beef into 1 in. cubes. Place them in two pints of water and bring to boil. Skim all scum and impurities away thoroughly. Place pan on an asbestos mat and simmer over a very low heat for one and a half hours. Cut turnips into ½ in. cubes. Add them to the beef broth together with sliced ginger. Boil gently for thirty minutes. Add all the seasonings. Stir and serve.

15. PURE BEEF BROTH

1 lb. beef
2–3 slices of ginger
3 onions
2½ tsp. salt
3 tbsp. sherry
1 stock-cube

Clean and cut beef into inch cubes. Place in a pint of water in a saucepan and bring to boil for three minutes. Pour all this water, with its impurities, away. Place the beef in a double boiler with ginger, onion and salt. Pour two pints of boiling water on to the beef. Cover tightly and simmer over a very low heat for five hours. Season with stock-cube, pepper and serve.

16. VEGETARIAN SOUP

2 carrots
1 turnip
2 tomatoes
¼ cabbage
3 oz. pea-starch noodles
3 oz. bamboo shoots
3 oz. pea sprouts
2 spring onions
3 oz. Chinese pickled veg. (cha tsai)
1½ tbsp. veg. oil
2 tsp. salt
3 tbsp. Vesop
½ tsp. Ve-tsin
Pepper

Shred carrots, turnips, bamboo shoots and cabbage into match-stick strips. Fry them in oil with 1 tsp. of salt and the sliced tomatoes for five to six minutes. Pour into the fried mixed vegetables two pints of water. Add noodles. Boil gently for thirty minutes. Slice the pickled vegetables into $1\frac{1}{2}$ in slices. Add them, with pea sprouts and chopped spring onions into the vegetable broth. Stir and add the seasonings, continue to boil gently for ten minutes and serve.

Chapter Six

MEAT DISHES

When we say meat in China it generally means pork. This is probably due to the fact that, while all the other cattle can be put to some other uses, pigs are primarily reared for food. This does not, however, mean that mutton, beef and goat meat are not popular. Mutton is eaten extensively in the North and goat meat is popular in the South, where, among the hilly regions, probably more goats are raised.

The main reason why the cow is not so often killed for its meat is because it is the main beast of burden in the growing of rice. Besides, south of the Yangtse half of the cows one sees are water-buffaloes, which have the appearance more of the hippo and rhinoceros than the ordinary cow, and their meat is probably a little too tough for ordinary culinary purposes.

PORK

1. BRAISED LEG OF PORK

3–4 lb. leg of pork
½ cup (8 tbsp.) soya sauce
1½ cup water
4 tbsp. sherry
1½ tbsp. sugar

Clean the leg of pork, make a few slashes in the skin, and place in a heavy saucepan with water, soya sauce and sherry. Heat over a high fire until it starts to boil. Insert an asbestos mat and simmer over a very low fire for three hours. Turn the pork in the gravy two or three times during the process of cooking, so that the whole joint will become evenly brown. Add additional seasoning or water, if necessary, or if desired, and simmer for a further half hour. Serve whole in a large bowl or deep, hot plate.

The meat in this case, after the prolonged cooking, will have become so tender that it can, as it generally is in China, be pulled to pieces by a pair of chopsticks. In the West, the carving knife should move through the pork as if through butter. To the connoisseur the fat of the pork is no longer regarded as fat in the normal European way, but as a kind of rich sweet jelly, and can therefore be consumed in very considerable quantities, with great enjoyment and no ill effect. The rich brown gravy, when added to rice, produces such a succulent mixture that it is not far off the mark to describe it as the hungry rice-eater's dream of heaven.

2. CHINESE CASSEROLE OF PORK (Also known as Tung-po Pork, reputed to have been invented by the famous Tang Dynasty poet, Soo Tung-Po).

    4 lb. pork (belly)
    ¾ cup soya sauce
    4 tbsp. sherry
    1 tbsp. lard
    ½ tbsp. sugar
    2–3 slices of ginger

Cut the meat into 1 to 1½ in. pieces against the grain. Fry the pieces of meat in fat until brown. Place the meat in a heavy pot, pour in soya sauce and cook for a minute or two, stirring continually. Add ginger and one cup of boiling water. Bring to boil. Lower the fire and insert an asbestos sheet under the pan, and leave the pot, tightly covered, to simmer for one and a quarter hours. Add sherry, sugar, stir, and simmer for a further half hour.

This style of pork dish is capable of two further variations:

(1) On opening the pot after one and a half hours of simmering, use a ladle full of the fat and gravy of the pork to fry any of the following vegetables: (a) sliced cabbage; (b) spinach; (c) cauliflower. When cooked, after three to five minutes frying, place the vegetables at the bottom of a large bowl or deep plate (hot) and pour the cooked pork and gravy over the vegetables. This is one of the most common and popular pork dishes in China.

(2) The pork can also be cooked with whole hard-boiled eggs, turnips, abalone, salted fish (haddock or squid). These ingredients should be added at the beginning and cooked the full one and three-quarter hours with the pork.

3. WHITE CUT PORK

3 lb. pork (leg undercut)
2 tsp. chopped ginger
4 tbsp. soya sauce

Wash the meat and place in a pot. Pour in one and a half pints of water. Bring to boil and leave to simmer for forty-five minutes. Remove meat from pot and cut against grain into $\frac{1}{6}$ in. thin slices when cold. Arrange the pieces on a large plate. Serve with soya sauce and chopped ginger.

4. STEAM MINCED PORK WITH CAULIFLOWER

1 lb. pork (minced)
1 cauliflower
1 egg
1 tbsp. cornflour
1 medium-sized onion
1 tbsp. soya sauce
1 tsp. salt
$\frac{1}{2}$ tsp. sugar
1 tbsp. sherry

Mince pork finely and place it in a large bowl with beaten egg, salt, sugar, cornflour, chopped onion, soya sauce and sherry. Mix thoroughly. Meanwhile, cut the cauliflower into inch pieces and place them at the bottom of another basin. Pack the minced pork mixture over the cauliflower. Place the basin in a steamer and steam for forty minutes.

5. STEAMED PORK WITH SALTED FISH

$1\frac{1}{2}$ lb. pork
$\frac{1}{2}$ lb. salted fish
2 slices ginger (root)
1 tbsp. lard
2 tbsp. sherry
1 tsp. sugar

Cut salted fish into inch size pieces. Fry in fat until well brown and crispy. Place them in a large bowl with ginger and pork which has also been cut into 1½ in. size pieces against grain. Add soya sauce, sugar and sherry, and a quarter cup of water. Place the bowl or basin in a steamer and steam over a moderate heat for two hours.

6. STEAMED PORK WITH POWDERED RICE

1½ lb. pork
3 tbsp. soya sauce
3 tbsp. sherry
½ cup ground rice (roasted)
2 chopped onions
2 tsp. chopped ginger

·Cut pork into 1½ in. pieces. Mix them with soya sauce, sherry, sugar, chopped onions and chopped ginger. Now add ground rice and mix thoroughly. Steam the basin containing this mixture over a low heat for two hours.

7. FRIED PORK RIBBONS WITH YOUNG LEEKS
(Bamboo shoots, celery, pea-sprouts can also be used)

1 lb. pork
3 young leeks
½ tbsp. cornflour
1 egg
1 tsp. sugar
1½ tbsp. soya sauce
2 tbsp. vegetable oil
2 tbsp. chicken or pork broth

Wash leeks thoroughly and cut into $\frac{1}{2}$ inch sections. Cut pork against grain into $1\frac{1}{2}$ in. lengths and $\frac{1}{8}$ in. wide ribbons. Mix pork with beaten egg (half an egg will do) and cornflour. Fry the pork with leeks in vegetable oil over a high heat for five minutes, turning quickly and continually. Add soya sauce and stock and fry a further three minutes. Add the seasonings and continue to cook for two minutes. Serve immediately on a hot plate.

8. FRIED PORK RIBBONS WITH PICKLED VEGE- TABLES (Tsa Chai, or pickled cabbage, cucumber, etc.)

1 lb. pork
$\frac{1}{4}$ lb. pickled vegetables (chopped)
3 oz. bamboo shoots (shredded)
$\frac{1}{2}$ tbsp. cornflour
1 tsp. sugar
$1\frac{1}{2}$ tbsp. soya sauce
2 tbsp. vegetable oil
2 tbsp. stock
1 tbsp. sherry

Follow the preparations in the previous recipe. Both the bamboo shoots and pickled vegetables should be fried with the pork from the beginning, before adding soya sauce, stock and other seasoning. It is essential to fry over a high heat.

The resulting dish is one of the most savoury that can be prepared. The impregnation of the pork by the pickle and vice-versa, gives the dish a "strength" unknown in any other way of cooking.

9. FRIED SWEET AND SOUR SPARE RIBS

The use of rib-bone meat in the form of miniature chops, in which some twenty or thirty chops are served up together in a single dish seems to be a distinctively Chinese conception.

> *3 lb. spare ribs (with plenty of meat)*
> *1 egg*
> *1 tbsp. cornflour*
> *2 tbsp. soya sauce*
> *2 tbsp. sherry*
> *4 tbsp. vegetable oil*

Cut the bones apart by cutting through the meat in between the bones. Chop the bone (and meat) into 1 in. length pieces. Soak them in a mixture of soya sauce and sherry for half an hour. After the seasoning, mix the bones with beaten egg and flour with cornflour. Fry the chops in oil for five minutes over high heat, and drain.

Meanwhile, prepare the SWEET AND SOUR SAUCE as follows:

Use 2 oz. pickles, 2 onions, 3 skinned tomatoes, 2 tbsp. vegetable oil, ½ cupful of stock, 3 tbsp. soya sauce, 2 tbsp. sugar, 2 tbsp. vinegar, 1 tbsp. cornflour and ¼ cup of water. *Pineapples*

Fry the mixed vegetables and pickles in the oil for five minutes. Add the stock, soya sauce, sugar and vinegar, and simmer for ten minutes. Thicken by adding the cornflour dissolved in the water. Bring to the boil again and pour it over the fried spare ribs. Continue to fry for one minute and serve.

10. SWEET AND SOUR PORK

Repeat the same preparations as given in the previous recipe, only substitute pork cut in ¾ in. squares for spare ribs.

This is a popular dish in the majority of Western Chinese restaurants. Here the pieces of pork are often encased in thick batter, which has the disadvantage of absorbing too much fat when deep-fried. Plain sweet and sour pork is much easier to prepare than sweet and sour spare ribs, if only for the fact that meat is much easier to cut than bones. But fried rib bones is a much better, more classical Chinese dish – if only for the proverbial fact that "the nearer the bone the sweeter the meat".

11. FRIED DICED PORK WITH BAMBOO SHOOT, WATER CHESTNUTS AND SOYA BEAN PASTE
(or Sauce "cracked" diced pork with bamboo shoots, etc.)

1 lb. pork (lean)
1 egg
3 oz. bamboo shoots
1 tbsp. cornflour
3 oz. water chestnuts
1 tsp. sugar
2 cloves garlic
3 tbsp. vegetable oil
1 tbsp. sherry
2 tbsp. soya sauce paste
Pepper

Dice pork into ¼ in. cubes. Mix with beaten egg and flour

with cornflour. Fry in oil over high fire for five minutes. Add soya sauce paste and garlic, fry for a further two minutes.

Now add all the ingredients – diced bamboo shoots and diced water chestnuts, and the seasonings (sugar, salt, sherry, pepper) and continue to fry for four to five minutes.

Owing to the great heat of the frying the diced meat jumps and cracks in the pan, and this type of frying is known in China as cracked-fried.

12. SAUCE "CRACKED" DICED PORK WITH PIMENTO AND RED PEPPER

1 lb. pork
2 tbsp. soya sauce paste
1 large pimento
2 small red peppers
3 tbsp. vegetable oil
1 tsp. salt
1 tsp. sugar
1 egg
1 tbsp. cornflour
2 tbsp. chicken broth
1 tbsp. sherry

Prepare according to the previous recipes. Add pimento and red peppers which have been sliced into pieces 1 in. length and $\frac{1}{2}$ in. width, when the diced pork and soya sauce paste have been frying for two minutes. Add salt, sherry, broth and sugar and fry for a further four to five minutes. Toss and stir quickly all the time while frying. This is essential in all "cracked" frying.

13. FRIED KIDNEY WITH SPRING ONION AND CAULIFLOWER

2 pairs kidneys
½ medium sized cauliflower
3 spring onions
1½ tbsp. soya sauce
3 tbsp. lard
1 tsp. salt
1 tsp. sugar
1½ tbsp. sherry
1 tsp. chopped ginger

Slice kidneys into pieces 1½ in. long and ½ in. wide, after removing membrane and gristle. Cut a few criss-cross slashes on top of each piece. Soak them in sherry.

Cut cauliflower into pieces 1 in. square and put into a pan of boiling water to boil for three minutes.

Meanwhile mix the sherry-soaked kidney with 1 tbsp. soya sauce and cornflour. Fry them with sliced onions over a very fierce heat for one and a half minutes, stirring continually. Now add the cauliflower after draining off all water; also add the remainder of the soya sauce, cornflour, salt, sugar. Continue stirring briskly and fry a further two minutes. Serve very hot.

14. FRIED LIVER WITH SPRING ONIONS AND LEEKS

1 lb. liver
2 leeks
1 spring onion
2 tbsp. lard

2 tbsp. soya sauce
1 tbsp. cornflour
1 tsp. sugar
1 tsp. salt
2 tbsp. sherry

Cut liver into slices 1½ in. in length. Soak for one minute
in boiling water to seal their outside layer. Strain off all
water. Mix with cornflour, sherry and soya sauce. Wash
leeks and slice into 1 in. sections. First fry liver in very
hot fat for one minute. Add leeks and continue to fry and
stir for two minutes. Add all the remaining seasonings.
Continue to stir briskly for two minutes. Serve very hot.

BEEF DISHES

1. FRIED BEEF RIBBONS WITH ONION (OR YOUNG LEEKS)

1 lb. beef (steak)
4 medium sized onions (leeks)
½ tbsp. cornflour (blend with 2 tbsp. chicken stock)
2 tbsp. fat or vegetable oil
2½ tbsp. soya sauce
1 tsp. sugar
1½ tbsp. sherry
Pepper and salt to taste

Clean beef and slice into 1½ in. long and ⅛ in. wide strips
or ribbons. Mix with cornflour mixture. Slice onions into
about ¼ in. width pieces.

Fry beef in oil for one minute, tossing and turning continually. Add onion and fry a further one and a half minutes. Add all the seasonings and sherry, salt and pepper to taste. Fry over a high heat for a further two minutes. Remove from heat and serve immediately.

2. SLICED BEEF FRIED WITH TOMATOES

1 lb. beef (steak)
4 tomatoes
1 tbsp. tomato purée
1 egg
½ tbsp. cornflour
2 tbsp. peanut oil
1 tsp. salt
1 tsp. sugar
1 tbsp. soya sauce
1 tbsp. sherry
Pepper to taste

Cut beef against grain into thin slices. Mix with beaten egg and cornflour.

Cut tomatoes into thin slices. Salt them and fry for two minutes, remove from heat but keep warm.

Fry the sliced beef over a high heat with minced ginger, crushed garlic, for one minute. Add tomato purée and soya sauce. Stir for a further one minute. Now mix the fried tomatoes in with the beef in the pan. Continue to fry for one and a half minutes. Pepper and serve.

3. BEEF FRIED IN OYSTER SAUCE

1 lb. beef (steak)
1½ tbsp. oyster sauce
1 tbsp. soya sauce
1 onion
2 tbsp. vegetable oil (peanut or olive)
1 tsp. sugar
1 tsp. salt pepper
1 tbsp. sherry

Cut beef against grain into 1½ in. by 2 in. thin slices, season by soaking in sherry and soya sauce for half an hour. Heat oil in pan until very hot. Put the seasoned beef in and fry over a high heat, stirring briskly, for one minute. Now add sugar and oyster sauce. Stir and cook for a further minute. Serve immediately.

4. SPICED VELVETEEN OF BEEF

2 lb. steak
½ cup of soya sauce
½ cup of sherry
2 cups chicken broth
6 tbsp. lard
½ tsp. aniseed powder

Cut beef into eight pieces and fry in a saucepan for two to three minutes with 2 tbsp. lard, until slightly brown. Add chicken broth, sherry and soya sauce. Boil gently until the pan is almost dry and meat extremely tender. Remove from heat.

When cold, mince the meat, then place the mince in a pan with 4 tbsp. lard and fry over a very low heat, stirring continually. Fry, never forgetting to stir unceasingly, until the beef is completely dry (about thirty to forty minutes). Remove and pack the velvety beef into a jar or any sterilised container. This extraordinary dish is taken at breakfast with Congee, or for garnishing any plain white dish, or served as an hors d'oeuvres (*after* a banquet). In the West it can be used with excellent effect as cocktail canapés.

MUTTON AND LAMB

1. STEWED MUTTON WITH TURNIPS

> 1½ lb. leg of mutton
> 1 lb. turnips
> 2 slices of ginger
> 1½ tsp. salt.
> 3 tbsp. sherry

Cut meat into large chunks of about 1½ in. square. Boil in three cups of water for one minute. Pour all the water and impurities away. Place the meat now in a double-boiler, together with ginger and turnips cut into similar sized pieces. Bring to boil and simmer for two hours. Add salt and sherry and simmer for a further half hour.

2. FRIED THIN-SLICED MUTTON WITH LEEKS
(or onion)

1 lb. leg of mutton
3 leeks (or onions)
2 cloves crushed garlic
1 tsp. salt
1 tbsp. soya sauce
1 tbsp. sherry
2 tbsp. lard

Cut the mutton into very thin slices, about 2 in. long and
1 in. wide. Cut leeks (or onions) across grain into ½ in.
sections.

Fry the sliced mutton over a very high heat for one
minute. Add sliced leeks, garlic, soya sauce, sherry, and
stir briskly for two minutes. Serve very hot.

3. FRIED RIBBONS OF LAMB WITH PEA SPROUTS
AND SPRING ONIONS

1 lb. lamb meat
2 spring onions
1 cup pea sprouts
½ tbsp. cornflour
2 cloves of crushed garlic
1 tsp. salt
1 tbsp. soya sauce
2 tbsp. sherry

Cut lamb meat into thin slices and then cut further
into strips or ribbons. Mix thoroughly with flour. Cut
spring onions into 1½ in. sections. Fry lamb and onions in

fat over a high heat with garlic and salt, for two minutes.
Add pea sprouts, soya sauce and sherry. Fry and stir
briskly for a further two minutes. Pepper and serve very
hot.

Chapter Seven

CHICKEN AND POULTRY

1. STEAMED OR BOILED CHICKEN

1 medium sized chicken (boiler or roaster)
2 onions (sliced)
2–3 slices of ginger
½ tbsp. salt
4 tbsp. sherry

Clean the chicken thoroughly and place it whole in a double-boiler (or simply a large basin inside a larger saucepan one-third full of water) with ginger, onions and salt. Bring to boil and leave to simmer for two hours. Add sherry and continue to simmer for one more hour. The chicken should be ready to serve when the meat has become tender enough to be pulled to pieces easily by a chopstick or a blunt fork.

This is one of the most common forms in which chicken is eaten in China. It can be served in this manner whether in home cooking or at an ordinary banquet. It is generally served in a large bowl or a deep dish and the chicken is partly immersed in its own soup.

Apart from the ease with which the bird can be cooked in this manner, it is also considered very digestible and nutritious. Hence it is often used by invalids or expectant mothers.

2. WHITE CUT CHICKEN

1 young chicken
2 spring onions
2–3 slices of ginger
½ tbsp. salt

Clean the chicken thoroughly. Boil three pints of water in a saucepan. Add salt. Put the chicken, ginger and onions in the pan and boil for five to six minutes. Remove from fire and leave the contents of the pan to cool while tightly covered. When cold cut the chicken into pieces and serve them on a plate with a sprinkle of soya sauce and sesame oil.

3. DEEP-FRIED SPRING CHICKEN

1 large spring chicken
2 spring onions
flour
6 tbsp. soya sauce
6 tbsp. sherry
1 tsp. sugar
1 lb. lard

Clean the chicken thoroughly and chop it into a dozen or sixteen pieces. Place the cut chicken in a bowl and add soya sauce, sherry, sugar, chopped onions. Let the mixture stand for over an hour, and then dip each piece of chicken in flour so that it is well covered. Fry the chicken in hot fat over a brisk heat for about four to five minutes until golden brown. Drain and serve with a sprinkle of salt and pepper.

4. BRAISED CHICKEN

> *1 medium sized chicken*
> *2–3 slices of ginger*
> *2 spring onions*
> *½ cup of soya sauce*
> *1 tsp. sugar*
> *4 tbsp. sherry*
> *3 tbsp. vegetable oil (peanut or olive)*

Clean the chicken thoroughly and fry it in oil for four or five minutes in a saucepan. Now add one cup of boiling water, soya sauce, ginger, onion. Bring to boil again quickly, and leave to simmer for one hour with the lid on. Turn the chicken now and then during the process of cooking so as to get evenly brown. After one hour add sugar and sherry and continue to simmer for another twenty-five minutes. This chicken is served whole in a large bowl, and cut or taken to pieces with a pair of chopsticks on the table.

5. DICED CHICKEN MEAT FRIED WITH WALNUT

> *½ large young chicken*
> *1 cupful of walnuts*
> *4 mushrooms*
> *2 tbsp. soya paste*
> *½ tbsp. cornflour*
> *1 tbsp. sherry*
> *1 tsp. salt*
> *1 tsp. sugar*
> *½ cup vegetable oil (peanut or olive)*

Shell and dice the walnuts. Dice the chicken, dice the mushrooms (all to about $\frac{1}{4}$ in. square). Fry the walnuts first in oil until they are golden brown. Remove from fire, drain them of oil and place them on thick Manila paper, which will abosrb any remaining oil.

Fry the diced chicken meat in 3 tbsp. of oil over a brisk heat. (This is another case of "crack" frying). Stir for one minute or so and add cornflour, sugar, sherry, soya paste, having first of all mixed all the ingredients thoroughly.

Now add the diced mushrooms, which have been soaked in water for ten minutes. Fry and stir for a further three minutes. Remove from heat. Serve the contents of the frying-pan immediately with deep-fried walnuts, on a hot plate.

6. DICED CHICKEN FRIED WITH ASSORTED INGREDIENTS

   2 breasts of chicken
   4 mushrooms
   3 oz. water chestnuts
   3 oz. bamboo shoots
   3 oz. almonds
   2 spring onions
   3 oz. green peas
   3 tbsp. sherry
   3 tbsp. soya sauce
   4 tbsp. peanut (or olive oil)
   1 tbsp. cornflour

Dice the chicken meat (into $\frac{1}{4}$ in. cubes) and mix with sherry, soya sauce and cornflour, and chopped spring onions.

Soak almonds in hot water, remove inner skin. Fry them in oil for one minute or so until slightly brown and crisp, and remove from fire. Keep crispy and hot.

Use the same oil to fry mushrooms, water chestnuts and bamboo shoots (all diced to the same size as the chicken meat). Fry with salt for two minutes and remove from heat.

Meanwhile, fry the seasoned, diced chicken meat separately over a brisk heat for two minutes. Now add the already fried mushrooms, water chestnuts, bamboo shoots, and the remaining soya sauce (1 tbsp.) and sugar and stir briskly for one minute.

Serve the mixture immediately with fried almonds on a hot dish.

7. DEEP FRIED PAPER-WRAPPED CHICKEN

2 cut pieces of chicken (about ½ lb.)
2 spring onions
1 tbsp. chopped ginger
2 tbsp. soya sauce
1 tbsp. sherry
½ tsp. sugar
½ tsp. salt
Pepper
2 cups of vegetable oil or fat
16–20 pieces of cellophane paper (4 in. by 4 in.)

Remove bones and skin of chicken and cut into 1½ in. long slices. Mix soya sauce, chopped ginger, salt, sugar and pepper in a bowl and soak the sliced chicken in the mixture for half an hour. Now place each piece of chicken on a piece of cellophane paper and wrap securely in parcel fashion (with tongue tucked in).

Heat up the oil and fry the packages in it, in a deep frying-pan, over a brisk fire, for two and a half minutes. Serve the packages of chicken without unwrapping, after draining them of oil. The packages should be unwrapped by the diner only on the point of eating. The wrapper helps to hold the flavour and heat in the pieces of chicken.

8. SMOKED CHICKEN

1 medium sized chicken
6 spring onions
½ cup soya sauce
3 tbsp. brown sugar
3 tbsp. sherry
1 tbsp. salt
3 tbsp. fat

Clean and cut the chicken into ten or twelve pieces. Place the cut chicken in a saucepan with two cups of water, three sliced onions, salt, and simmer for half an hour. Add soya sauce and sherry, and continue to simmer for another half an hour.

Remove the chicken from the pan. Allow a little while for it to stand and dry. Now place the pieces on a grate or a perforated metal plate, which is in turn placed inside an iron pot, at the bottom of which is deposited 3 tbsp. brown sugar. Cover the pot tightly with a lid and place it over a fierce heat. Allow the chicken to be smoked inside the pot for five minutes.

Meanwhile, heat two tablespoons of fat and add to it two chopped onions and two tablespoons soya sauce. Fry the smoked pieces of chicken, together with them, for one and a half minutes and serve.

9. DRUNKEN DUCK

METHOD (*a*)

> 1 medium sized duck
> 2 spring onions
> ½ bottle cooking sherry
> 2–3 pieces ginger
> 2 tbsp. salt

Clean the duck thoroughly, removing all entrails.

Rub inside and outside with salt, and put chopped ginger and onion inside the bird. Then place it in a pot or heavy saucepan and simmer in sherry for one hour. Turn the bird every now and then in the process of the cooking. (It is advisable to use an asbestos mat to prevent burning). When cold remove bird from pot and cut into sixteen pieces. Serve on plate with spring onions cut into 2 in. sections.

METHOD (*b*)

> 1 medium sized duck
> ½ bottle cooking sherry
> 4 spring onions
> 2–3 pieces ginger
> 2 tbsp. salt

Pluck and wash the duck thoroughly. Place it in a heavy saucepan with salt and two pints of water, ginger and onions. Bring to boil and leave to simmer for forty minutes.

Remove from pot and leave to cool and dry. Now cut

the duck into sixteen pieces and place them in a basin or casserole. Pour sherry over them. Leave them to stand for five days to a week. A couple of hours before serving remove the duck from the sherry. Serve with spring onions cut into sections and sweet soya paste jam (if not available use blackcurrant jam).

10. WEST LAKE STEAMED DUCK (West Lake of Hangchow, the famous Lake District of China).

1 fat duck
1 small cabbage (large Chinese cabbage if available)
4 oz. ham
2 stalks of spring onions
6 tbsp. lard
1 tbsp. salt

Pluck and clean the duck thoroughly. Stuff the inside with onions, ham and salt. Tie or sew up securely. Fry the duck whole for ten to fifteen minutes until slightly brown. Remove from fat and place the duck in a large basin with cabbage. Place the basin in a large saucepan, one-third filled with water. Simmer continuously for three hours.

11. ROAST DUCK

1 fat duck
½ bottle cooking sherry
1 tbsp. honey
3 tbsp. soya sauce

Pluck and clean the duck thoroughly. Place it in a large saucepan with salt and sherry. Cook over a low heat for thirty minutes. Remove bird from pan and smear over with soya sauce. Place it in oven and roast for fifteen minutes at moderate heat. Remove from oven. Now smear the bird with honey (mixed with a little water) and soya sauce. Roast for another fifteen minutes at high temperature. Serve with blackcurrant jam, if sweet soya jam is not available.

Chapter Eight

VEGETABLES

The Chinese are great vegetable eaters. Like the French, or even more so, we regard many vegetable dishes as savouries in their own right, which are prepared by eminent chefs with great care and pride. Sliced and shredded vegetables, as the reader has already noted, are often cooked with meat and are impregnated with the meat taste, but even when cooked on their own they can be extremely tasty, as usually very little or no water is used in their cooking. When frying such vegetables as spinach, lettuce and watercress, no water is used at all, as the vegetables contain quite sufficient water to cook in their own juice. By cooking rapidly – generally in a couple of minutes – without using a lid to close the pan (whether a frying-pan or a sauce-pan is used) the crispness and green colour of the vegetable can be retained, or even enhanced. The lid is used only in cooking hard vegetables. More often hard vegetables are first fried for two or three minutes, and then water or stock is added together with seasonings, and cooking is carried on for a few more minutes. Thus the vegetable is partly fried and partly braised. Alternatively, a vegetable can be boiled for a minute or two before frying, particularly when the frying is intended to be of extremely short duration, such as one minute, although over a very brisk heat.

Those Westerners who have encountered Chinese food for the first time, are usually most impressed by Chinese vegetable dishes, for these have generally all the positive qualities, such as freshness, crispness, excellent colour, savouriness, and seldom tumble into any of the pitfalls which might confound or repel the uninitiated. Chinese vegetarian cooking is a very fascinating and large world of its own, which should provide an extremely interesting subject of research. It has grown and developed for a couple of thousand years, with Buddhism in China, and around the Buddhist temples and monasteries, which took pride in their culinary products. For its refinements and vastness of repertoire there is probably no parallel in the world.

1. FRIED SPINACH

1½ lb. spinach
2 lb. lard (or butter)
1 tsp. salt
1 tbsp. soya sauce

Wash the spinach thoroughly and drain it carefully of all water. Cut the leaves to about 3 in. lengths if they are very large, otherwise use them as they are. Heat the fat, preferably in a saucepan, until it spreads and covers the whole of the bottom of the pan. Put the spinach into the pan and fry over a brisk heat with salt for two and a half minutes. When the spinach has turned soft add soya sauce and continue to fry for two minutes.

2. CREAM SAVOURY CABBAGE

1 lb. white cabbage (Chinese if available)
2 tbsp. lard ·
½ cup stock
½ cup milk
2 tbsp. Vesop
2 oz. dried prawns (if available)
1 oz. minced ham
1 tbsp. sherry
½ tsp. Ve-tsin (or 1 chicken stock cube)
1 tsp. salt
Pepper

Choose a white cabbage. Wash and cut it into 2 in. squares. Cook in boiling water for three to four minutes and drain.

Meanwhile, fry the dried prawns in a saucepan for one and a half minutes. Add the cabbage and fry for two more minutes. Mix Ve-tsin with stock and pour it onto the cabbage. Cook and stir for ten minutes. Mix corn-flour with milk and add to the pan. Stir and simmer for ten more minutes. Sprinkle with minced ham and pepper on top. Serve in a deep vegetable dish with gravy.

3. BRAISED TURNIPS (OR CARROTS)

1 lb. turnips
2 tbsp. lard
1 spring onion
2 tbsp. soya sauce
2 tbsp. meat gravy (pork or beef)
1 tsp. sugar

Peel the turnips and cut them into $\frac{1}{2}$ in. wedges. Heat the lard in the pan and fry the diced turnips in it for four minutes. Pour in half cup of stock or water and leave to simmer for five minutes with lid on. Add soya sauce, meat gravy, chopped onion and sugar. Cook for ten more minutes. Pepper and serve.

This is a useful vegetable dish to have when there is not enough meat to go round, as it gives a slight illusion of meat.

4. FRIED LETTUCE

1 lettuce
2 tbsp. lard (or butter)
2 cloves of smashed garlic
$\frac{1}{2}$ tsp. salt
1 tbsp. Vesop (or soya sauce)

Wash the lettuce thoroughly. Cut into 2 in. pieces. Melt the fat and put the crushed garlic into the pan and fry for half a minute. Add lettuce, sprinkle with salt and fry for one minute. Add Vesop, fry and turn the lettuce for half a minute and serve.

5. FRIED MUSHROOMS AND BAMBOO SHOOTS WITH MINCED HAM

12 mushrooms
$\frac{1}{2}$ lb. bamboo shoots
1 tbsp. cornflour
3 tbsp. lard (or butter)
$1\frac{1}{2}$ tbsp. sherry
1 tbsp. Vesop (or soya sauce)
$\frac{1}{2}$ tsp. salt

Wash the mushrooms and soak in half a cup of boiling water for one hour before cooking. Fry the mushrooms in half the lard for two minutes and remove from pan. Cut the bamboo shoots into slices and fry in remaining lard with salt and sherry for five minutes. Now add the cooked mushrooms and pour in the Vesop and sherry and stir for one minute. Add the mushroom water from the cup and simmer for ten minutes. Meanwhile, mix cornflour with a little water; the mixture is then added to the pan. Sprinkle the mixture with minced ham and bring to quick boil.

When serving arrange the mushrooms over the bamboo shoots on a plate and pour the creamy gravy over them.

6. BROWN BRAISED CABBAGE WITH MUSH-ROOMS

1 small cabbage
2 oz. dried prawns
2 tbsp. lard
4 mushrooms
2 tbsp. soya sauce
1 tsp. sugar
1 tsp. Ve-tsin (or 1 chicken stock cube)

Melt lard in the frying-pan. Fry the dried shrimps in it for two minutes. Cut the cabbage into eight pieces, and boil in two cups of water for ten minutes. Drain, add to the shrimps and fry for three to four minutes. Add half the cabbage water, bring to boil and leave to simmer for ten minutes. Add soya sauce, sugar, stock cube, sliced mushrooms and simmer for a further ten minutes.

7. SWEET AND SOUR CABBAGE

1 cabbage
3 tomatoes
1 carrot
3 tbsp. lard
1½ tbsp. sherry
1½ tbsp. cornflour (blended in ½ cup of water)
2 tbsp. vinegar
2 tbsp. sugar
2 tbsp. soya sauce

Prepare the sweet and sour sauce by frying shredded carrots and sliced tomatoes in 1½ tsp. of lard for five minutes. Add vinegar, sugar and soya sauce, and pour into the pan half a cup of water in which the cornflour has been mixed. Bring to boil and stir until the mixture is thick.

Meanwhile, cut the cabbage into 1½ in. squares. Fry in the remaining lard for four to five minutes over a brisk heat. Add sherry during the last minute of frying. Pour the sweet and sour sauce in and leave to cook for two minutes.

This is a useful dish to serve with roast pork and the like, if eaten with European food.

8. ONION SAUCE

4 onions
½ tbsp. sugar
2 tbsp. soya sauce
1½ tbsp. lard

Slice the onion and fry in lard for four minutes. Add sugar and soya sauce and fry for a further two minutes. Stir and turn briskly while frying.

A very convenient and useful sauce to have for serving with steaks and chops.

9. CHINESE VEGETABLE SALAD

1 stick celery
1 lettuce
1 carrot
½ cucumber
⅛ cabbage
3 cloves garlic
1 tbsp. Vesop
2 tbsp. salad oil
1 tbsp. vinegar
1 tbsp. soya sauce
2 tsp. sesame oil

Dice the celery, shred the cabbage, grate the carrot, crush the garlic, slice the cucumber. Mix these together first with Vesop and soya sauce and then with salad, sesame oils and vinegar and serve on top of lettuce leaves.

This is, of course, a dish invented by the Chinese for the benefit of foreigners, as in China, at least in the past, if you indulged in uncooked vegetables, which had been freshly manured you'd be dead with cholera, typhoid, dysentery and numerous other famous diseases before you could say Chinese mayonnaise.

Perhaps it should be noted here that the Chinese are so confident of their own culinary art that, like the English men of letters who think nothing of incorporating Latin, French or German expressions into their own language, the Chinese chefs have no qualms whatsoever in incorporating Western methods into Chinese cooking. Much as English literature is enriched by European influence, so has Chinese cooking been enriched through the ages by Mogul, Mohammedan, Indian, Japanese and European influence. Because of the vast entity of Chinese cooking, everything that is introduced is immediately assimilated. It has no self-consciousness in the use of methods which were not originally Chinese.

Chapter Nine

FISH AND SHELL-FISH

It is strange to say that in China, a continental country with little refrigeration, the fish supplied are, as a rule, fresher than those one finds in this country. For half the time they are supplied alive. All better-class restaurants keep their fish, not dead in refrigerators, but alive in large jars (like those one reads of in the stories of Aladdin) or in tanks. With a coastline of over three thousand miles, several of the world's mighty rivers and thousands of streams, tributaries and lakes, naturally all types of fish abound. Added to all these sources of supply, we Chinese also "farm" fish from artificial pools. Fish farming is certainly as widely practised in China as dairy farming is in this country. So almost every village has a small lake or pool as an inherent part of its scenery or man-made landscape, and all sorts of waste and feeding-stuffs are thrown into it to feed and multiply the fish.

What of the sea fish? These are eaten either very soon after they are caught, or they are preserved, cooked, or salted. While fresh or cooked fish prepared in the Chinese way, using wine and ginger to disguise any of the less agreeable flavours, is very palatable and easily acceptable to the Westerner, they have to be warned in so far as Chinese salted fish is concerned. The normal way in which we Chinese treat this type of fish is to fry it until even the bones are crispy (and melting) which makes it a first-class accompaniment to plain rice. But during the process of thorough frying, to the practised nostril a very

beautiful and all-pervading aroma permeates the area
within fifty yards of the frying, which to the average
uninitiated Westerner, unless aided by a vast stretch
of imagination, is just undeniable stink. Unless your
neighbours are more humorously inclined than can be
believed, or you fry with the greatest circumspection,
such as in an airtight chamber, they are sooner or later
bound to obtain a court injunction against you con-
tinuing in your repulsive habits, which amounts to being
a public nuisance and may affect the respectability and
rateable value of the area in which you reside.

So should you ever be invited to a Chinese home and,
whilst you wait for the meal to be served, you smell an
unmentionable smell, filling the room, don't be alarmed.
It is only salted fish being fried. The Chinese attraction to
salted fish is much the same as an Englishman's inclination to ripe cheeses. Indeed the two things belong to the
same category.

In the following recipes given below you will, however,
be treading on perfectly safe ground.

1. STEAMED FISH (WHOLE)

1 fish (perch, bass, carp, etc.)
6 mushrooms
2 spring onions
2 slices ham
4 slices of ginger
2 tbsp. soya sauce
1 tsp. salt
1 tbsp. lard
1 tbsp. sherry
½ tsp. sugar

Clean and scale the fish, and rub both inside and out with salt. Place it in a long dish or basin. Add soya sauce, sherry, sugar and shredded ginger. Arrange the mushrooms, ham and onions cut in 2 in. lengths nicely on top. Place the dish in a steamer and steam in a good heat for thirty minutes.

2. STEAMED FISH IN SLICES

1 lb. fish (plaice, sole, halibut, turbot, etc.)
6 mushrooms
2 slices ginger
2 slices ham
1½ tbsp. sherry
1 tbsp. vinegar
1 tbsp. soya sauce
2 tbsp. lard
1 tsp. salt
½ tsp. sugar

Wash and cut the fish into 2 in. length slices. Rub with salt and place in a dish or basin with white side up.

Meanwhile, mix the various ingredients together – chopped spring onions, soya sauce, sugar, vinegar, sherry – pour them over the sliced fish. Place some bits of sliced ham and sliced mushrooms over each piece of fish. Put the dish or basin in a steamer and steam for twenty-five minutes. Season with some pepper and serve.

3. DEEP FRIED FISH (IN PIECES)

1 lb. fish (cod, halibut, haddock)
1 lb. lard

1½ tbsp. flour
1 egg
1 tsp. salt

Clean fish and cut into 1 in. wide by 2 in. length pieces. Rub them with salt. Mix flour with beaten egg and add two spoonfuls of water. Coat the fish with this thin flour-egg paste.

Heat and bring the lard to boil. Drop the pieces of fish into it, a few at a time. Remove and drain when slightly brown. Serve on a hot plate with salt and pepper.

Small fish like sprats and herring can be cooked in this manner whole. They should be fried until quite brown, so that the head and tails will have become crispy.

4. SLICED FISH IN SWEET AND SOUR SAUCE

1 lb. fish (sole, plaice, turbot, halibut, etc.)
1 lb. lard
2–3 tomatoes
2 oz. pickles
1 tbsp. cornflour
2 tbsp. vinegar
1½ tbsp. sugar
2 tbsp. soya sauce
6 tbsp. stock (bone)

Prepare sweet and sour sauce as in sweet and sour pork or sweet and sour cabbage (Pages 58 and 81).

Cut fish into 2 in. length and 1½ in. wide slices. Rub with salt. Coat the pieces of fish with a mixture of flour and water. Fry until slightly brown. Remove from pan and drain off oil. Place the pieces on a hot plate. Heat the sweet and sour sauce until boiling, and pour it over the sliced fish.

5. BRAISED EEL

1 lb. eel
2 spring onions
3 cloves garlic
1 tsp. cornflour
2 tbsp. soya sauce
3 lb. lard
2 tbsp. sherry
2 tsp. sugar
½ tsp. salt

Clean and cut the eel into 2 in. sections. Heat lard and fry the eel in it with chopped onion for five minutes. Add sherry, soya sauce, sugar, garlic, salt and finally a cup of water. Leave to simmer for fifteen to twenty minutes. Stir in cornflour mixed with water. Pepper, bring to boil and serve.

6. BRAISED FISH (Carp, Bream, Perch, Halibut, Haddock, Cod)

2 lb. fish
2 spring onions
3–4 slices ginger
3 tbsp. soya sauce
1 oz. ham
4 tbsp. lard
2 tbsp. sherry
2 tsp. sugar
1 tsp. salt

Scale the fish (if whole) and wash it carefully. Stand for a while to dry, and rub it over with salt. Fry it for about five minutes and baste it continually while frying. Now pour the soya sauce evenly over the fish. Add ginger, chopped spring onion, ham, and braise for a few minutes until the seasonings have penetrated the fish.

Add ½ cup of water. Bring contents to boil again. Add sugar and sherry. Leave to simmer for fifteen minutes.

Cooked in this manner, not only will the frying and stewing have eliminated all fishy smell, but the gravy of the fish is extremely tasty.

7. PRAWNS FRIED IN SHELLS

1 lb. prawns
4 tbsp. lard
2 spring onions
2 cloves smashed garlic
2 tbsp. soya sauce
2 tbsp. sherry
1 tsp. vinegar
1 tsp. sugar
½ tsp. salt

Trim the whiskers and tails of the prawns with a pair of scissors. Wash in water and drain thoroughly.

Heat the lard in a frying-pan. Fry the prawns in it for about two minutes over a medium heat. Turn the heat higher; add all the ingredients (chopped onion and garlic) at once, as well as all the seasonings. Fry for a further two and a half minutes and serve immediately. (This is a favourite dish in Peking during the summer, when the prawns attain almost the size of small lobsters).

8. FRIED SHELLED PRAWNS WITH PEA SPROUTS

1 lb. prawns
3 tbsp. lard
6 oz. pea sprouts
1½ tbsp. soya sauce
2½ tbsp. sherry
½ tsp. salt
½ tsp. sugar

Shell the prawns, wash and drain thoroughly. Season the prawns in salt for one hour before cooking.

Heat the lard in the frying-pan, and fry the prawns in it for two minutes with salt. Add the pea shoots and fry for one minute. Now add all the other seasonings – sugar, salt, soya sauce, sherry – and fry for a further two minutes, tossing and stirring continually as you fry. Serve with a little pepper.

9. DEEP FRIED LOBSTER

2 lb. fresh lobster
1 egg
6 tbsp. lard
2 tbsp. cornflour
1 tsp. salt

Clean and boil the lobsters for three minutes. Remove the meat from the shells. Cut the lobster meat into ½ in pieces. Dip them in batter made from beaten egg, cornflour, 1 tbsp. of water and a little salt.

Heat the lard to boiling and drop the lobsters into it to fry for three minutes, or until they are golden brown. Pepper and serve.

10. BRAISED LOBSTER WITH EGG AND PORK

3 lobsters
2 eggs
¼ lb. lean pork
1 tsp. chopped ginger
1 spring onion
1 tbsp. soya sauce
2 tbsp. sherry
½ tbsp. cornflour
½ tsp. salt
1 tsp. sugar

Clean and cut the lobsters lengthwise and then into 1½ in. sections with shells on. Fry in lard and salt over a high fire for two minutes. Add shredded pork and fry a further two minutes.

Beat the eggs and mix thoroughly with chopped ginger, onions, soya sauce, sugar, sherry, cornflour and 3 tbsp. of water. Steam the mixture in a very thin steam over the lobster in the pan, stir and toss over high heat for three more minutes.

11. CRAB MEAT IN STEAM EGGS

1 large crab
2 eggs
2 spring onions
1 tbsp. soya sauce
2 tbsp. sherry
1 tsp. salt
1 tbsp. lard

Wash and steam the crab for fifteen minutes. Remove the meat from the shell.

Beat the eggs, mix them with salt, soya sauce, chopped onion. Add crab meat, sherry and half a cupful of water. Mix thoroughly. Add lard. Steam for twenty minutes. The dish is cooked when it attains the semi-solid form of a custard. When serving the basin or dish used is brought in steaming and placed on the dining-table itself. This dish goes well with plain rice and braised pork and is served with soya sauce sprinkled over the egg.

12. FRIED ABALONE (OR AWABI) WITH OYSTER SAUCE

1 tin abalone
4 tbsp. oyster sauce
1 slice ham (chopped)
1 tbsp. soya sauce
½ tbsp. corn starch
1 tbsp. lard

Remove the abalone from the tin, but keep the abalone water in a cup. Cut the abalone into slices 1 in. square and about ¼ in. thick. Heat lard in a pan and fry the abalone in it for half a minute. Add oyster sauce and soya sauce. Stir for half a minute. Mix corn starch in abalone water and pour it into the pan. Cook for not more than one and a half minutes over a high fire. Garnish with chopped ham and serve.

13. PRAWN FU-YUNG (EGG-WHITE)

1 lb. prawns (shelled)
6 eggs

3 slices ginger
1 tbsp. sherry
1 tsp. soya sauce
4 tbsp. lard
½ tsp. salt

Shell and wash the prawns. Separate the egg-white from the yoke. Beat up the egg-white and mix the prawns in with it. Add the seasoning and mix thoroughly.

Heat the lard in the pan until boiling. Pour the prawn mixture into the pan, stir and toss over a brisk heat for three to four minutes. Pepper and serve on a hot plate.

14. DRUNKEN SHRIMPS

1 lb. fresh shrimps
2 tsp. chopped ginger
½ cupful sherry
2 tbsp. soya sauce
1 tsp. salt
1 tsp. vinegar

Choose the freshest shrimps (if possible alive). Trim off tails and whiskers. Wash carefully. Place the shrimps in a deep basin. Sprinkle with salt, soya sauce and ginger. Mix well.

An hour later add sherry and vinegar. Stand for a further hour, drain and serve.

Chapter Ten

EGGS

In China eggs are more often used as ingredients in conjunction with other foods rather than independently, but there are a number of useful recipes:

1. EGG OMELET WITH ASSORTED INGREDIENTS

> 6 eggs
> ¼ lb. shredded pork meat (chicken, crab or shrimps can also be used)
> 4 oz. pea sprouts
> 2 spring onions
> 4 tbsp. oil (or lard)
> 2 tbsp. soya sauce
> 1 tbsp. sherry
> 1 tsp. salt
> ½ tbsp. sherry

Beat up the eggs with salt and put them aside.

Cut pork into shreds and spring onions into ½ in. sections. Fry them in 1 tbsp. hot fat for two and a half minutes, then add pea sprouts, sherry, soya sauce, and fry for a further one and a half minutes. Remove from pan, but keep hot.

Heat the remaining fat until it has spread completely over the bottom of the pan. Pour in the beaten eggs. Do not stir but lift the bottom of the egg occasionally to see that it does not stick. After about a minute, before the whole of the egg has hardened, add all the cooked shredded meat, spring onion, pea sprouts. After about half a minute fold the edges of the omelet over each other with the aid of a fish slice. Serve on a warm plate.

2. STEAMED EGGS AND MINCED MEAT

4 eggs
¼ lb. minced pork
1 oz. minced ham
1 spring onion, (chopped)
1 tsp. lard
1 tsp. soya sauce
1 tsp. salt
1 cup stock or milk

Beat the eggs up with minced pork, chopped onions, and salt. Place them in a deep bowl or basin with lard and half a cup of stock (bone) or milk. Mix well. Place the basin in a steamer or a large boiler, and steam for twenty minutes with lid on. Remove basin from steamer, pour the soya sauce over the now solidified custard-like mixture. Garnish with minced ham and serve on the table in the basin.

3. SCRAMBLED EGGS WITH SHRIMPS (OR PRAWNS)

6 eggs
½ lb. shrimps
2 spring onions (chopped)
2 mushrooms

3 tbsp. lard
3 tbsp. sherry
1 tsp. salt
Pepper to taste

Beat the eggs. Add salt, pepper, sherry and mix well.

Shell the shrimps, clean well. Fry them with chopped onion and sliced mushrooms in hot fat for one minute. Pour in the egg mixture. Stir and continue to fry and scramble for two to three minutes. This can be a highly appetising and aromatic dish.

4. BRAISED EGGS IN PORK GRAVY

6 eggs
1 lb. pork
½ cup soya sauce
2 tbsp. sherry
1 tsp. salt
1 tsp. sugar

Braise the pork in the usual way by cutting into 1 in. squares, simmer in a heavy pot or pan for one and a half hours with soya sauce, salt, sherry, sugar and half a cup of water, over a low heat.

Boil the eggs first for six to seven minutes and cool afterwards under cold tap-water. Now shell the eggs and place them carefully in the pan with braised pork. See that each egg is covered by the gravy. Resume simmering for a further half an hour.

Eggs braised in this manner can either be served whole, with braised pork or, as they are more often than not, served cold on their own, after they have been cut into quarters or sixes when they are cold, and arranged on a dish with the yoke side turned upwards – a favourite breakfast or late supper dish. They are often sold in market-stalls, as well as sampan-stalls, which ply along the river, selling both to the floating population and travellers who use the river as a highway.

5 HAM AND EGG DUMPLINGS

1 lb. ham
4 eggs
1 tsp. flour
3 slices of bread
1 lb. fat

Chop or mince the ham. Beat the eggs up thoroughly. Mix the eggs and ham up well together. Now rub the bread into crumbs and add them together with the flour to the egg and ham mixture to make a thick paste. Make the paste into balls about the size of pigeons' eggs. Heat the oil until boiling, and fry the ham-egg balls in it for four to five minutes, or until golden brown. Serve on a hot plate.

6. EGG-WRAPPED DUMPLINGS

½ lb. pork
2 spring onions
1 tsp. chopped ginger
3 tbsp. lard
2 tbsp. soya sauce
1 tsp. salt
1 tsp. sugar

Beat up the egg with salt. Mince the pork and mix with chopped onion and ginger and soya sauce. Heat 2 tbsp. lard in the pan. When it has all melted and spread over the pan place 1 tbsp. of beaten egg in the centre of the pan. Immediately follow by putting 1 tsp. of minced pork mixture in the centre of the egg. Fold over and press down the edges. Remove from pan and place it on a plate. Repeat the process until all the materials have been used up. When all the dumplings have been fried, add half a cup of stock to the pan together with sugar and soya sauce. Put back all the fried dumplings into the pan. Cover, and cook for five minutes and serve.

7. EGG THREADS (for garnishing)

3 eggs
3 tbsp. peanut oil

Best the eggs lightly. Heat the peanut oil in a frying-pan, then spread egg thinly over. Brown both sides of the egg. Cut the thin pancake into narrow strips. Repeat the process until all the eggs are used up. Keep the egg strips for use as garnish over various dishes, such as fried noodles and so on.

Chapter Eleven

SPECIALITIES

Among the various Chinese culinary specialities the best-known ones in the West are, of course, Shark's Fin and Bird's Nest Soups. Since we have already dealt with Bird's Nest Soup (under Soups), before coming to Shark's Fins, I think I shall introduce the reader to two other dishes which are more interesting and probably more satisfying. Having spent the last three hours involved in cooking and consuming the first of the following recipes, I can attest to the fact, from first-hand and more recent experience, that it is extremely filling!

1. "THE BOILING FIRE POT"

The literal translation of the Chinese name for this dish is "Fire Pot", but perhaps a more vivid and descriptive translation of what actually takes place on the table when this dish is being prepared and consumed would be "THE BOILING FIRE POT".

The main feature of this recipe is that the cooking of the food and eating of this dish proceed in a piecemeal manner, alternately and simultaneously, all on the dining-table. In other words, you eat as you cook, over a period of two to three hours. All the foods provided are prepared, but raw, and arranged in plates all around a round table (in the West a plastic top is necessary if the table is not to become stained). The essential equipment is a large round brass pot with a funnel running up the centre to about eighteen inches in height. At the bottom of this funnel and under the pot is an arrangement either for firing with charcoal, or burning with alcohol, thus sufficient heat can be generated to keep the pot in constant boil. The pot is generally lit and heated in the kitchen and is brought into the dining-room, and placed at the centre of the dining-table with its chinmey sprouting fire – a very warming sight during the winter months. Around the "Boiling fire pot" are arranged the following dishes and ingredients for a party of say, six to eight people.

(1) 2 plates full of thinly sliced chicken meat.

(2) 3 or 4 plates full of thinly sliced pork, lamb or beef (3 lb.).

(3) 2 plates full of thinly sliced fish (sole, plaice, turbot, halibut, etc.).

(4) $\frac{1}{4}$ lb. of Chinese pea-starch vermicelli, having been previously soaked in hot water for half an hour to soften.

(5) 6 spring onions, chopped into 1 in. sections.

(6) $\frac{1}{2}$ lb. spinach (carefully cleaned and washed).

(7) 2 plates full of thinly sliced liver (1 lb.).

(8) 1 pair of kidneys cleaned and sliced and placed on a plate.

(9) 1 large panful of hot chicken broth, or bone stock, for adding to the pot in the course of the dinner.

(10) $\frac{1}{2}$ lb. shredded cabbage.

The diner can either use a pair of chopsticks or simply a long fork and spoon. He picks up whatever food from one of the numerous plates he chooses – fish, flesh, fowl or vegetable, and dips it in that section of the boiling pot which is immediately in front of him, to cook. Since all the food and ingredients are very thinly sliced or shredded, and a big fire is kept up all the time, the food is immediately cooked in a matter of seconds. The diner thereupon quickly removes the food from the pot and dips it equally quickly in his own bowl, containing the mixed sauces (soya sauce, sesame oil, some chopped ginger or garlic, fermented soya bean paste, mixed to his own liking) before conveying it to his mouth. Rice is not generally served with the Boiling Fire Pot. The usual accompanying food used is the Chinese toasted cake, a bun-like baked cake, with sesame seeds studded on top, and less yeast and more salt used in the dough. Short of this, the ordinary Chinese steamed dumpling can also be used (in Europe one can just use bread or toasted bun).

As the meal progresses new platefuls of sliced meat and ingredients, as well as pans full of boiling stock are brought in from the kitchen to replenish any food which may have been finished. It is quite usual for such a meal to last two and a half to three hours, as so many different types of things can be cooked and eaten alternately at a sitting. The finale comes when the majority of the diners feel that they have had enough. Whereupon the soup in the pot, which by now is extremely tasty, owing to the fact that so much has been cooked in it, is conveyed to your sauce bowl in large spoonfuls, until you feel a balance is struck between the soup and the remaining sauce. You then lift the bowl to your mouth and drink it in a few big gulps. This last exertion produces that culminating sweat which is the height of gastronomic well-being: all this is, of course, a great help in warming the cockles of one's heart.

Both the "BOILING FIRE POT" and the "BRAZIER GRILLED

LAMB" are great favourites as winter pastimes in Peking.
There are several famous restaurants where nothing else
is served.

2. BRAZIER GRILLED SLICED LAMB

9 lb. leg of lamb (for six persons)
6 eggs
6 cloves crushed garlic (1 for each person)
6 chopped spring onions
6 tbsp. soya sauce
6 tbsp. fermented soya sauce
6 tbsp. sweet soya bean jam
3 tsp. chili sauce
3 tsp. sesame oil

For this dish a large open charcoal stove or brazier is
required, equipped with a well-meshed iron grate over the
top. The stove is brought in and placed on the centre of the
table after the charcoal has been fanned to blazing.

The mutton is sliced to paper thin slices, as in the
previous recipe, and arranged in plates around the charcoal burner. There should be at least three plates of meat
to each person, for meat is more easily consumed when
roasted than boiled. In front of each diner, as in the
previous recipe, there should be at least two bowls: one
containing a beaten egg and the other a mixture of the
various sauces (if sweet soya jam and fermented soya
paste are unavailable, blackcurrant jam and peanut
butter can be used as substitutes) together with chopped
onion and garlic.

Each diner uses a pair of long bamboo chopsticks
(bamboo because it does not matter so much when

damaged by burning). He picks up one or two pieces of sliced lamb meat and places it on the grate over the charcoal brazier. As the heat is so intense, the meat is cooked or roasted in a matter of seconds. Thereupon he removes the meat from the grate with his chopsticks and dips it quickly first into the beaten egg (partly to take on an interesting coating and partly to cool), and then immediately into the mixed sauces before conveying it to the watering mouth. As this process of grilling and eating is both fascinating and repetitive, and generates an appetite, often independent of whether the person is hungry or not, it is difficult to keep track of how much one has eaten. It is therefore, quite normal for a gentleman to consume say a dozen dishes of lamb at a sitting, so long as he doesn't take too much of the accompanying bread, which in this case, as in the previous recipe, is the Chinese toasted cake (in the West, ordinary toast or toasted French rolls can be served as a substitute).

3. SHARK'S FINS WITH CRAB MEAT

2 large crabs
¾ lb. skinless shark's fins
2 eggs
1 tsp. salt
3 tbsp. lard

Prepare the fins by soaking overnight in water, then steaming for two hours in a bowl of chicken broth which has been placed in a large pan of water, to simmer with lid on, so that the fins, originally as hard as raw hide, become completely soft.

Steam the crabs for half an hour. Scrape out all the

meat from the shell and claws. Heat the lard in a pan until boiling. Pour in crab meat mixed with the two beaten eggs. Add salt. Fry and stir for one minute.

Now add the softened shark's fin and fry for a further two minutes, with two or three spoonfuls of chicken broth.

4. SHARK'S FIN WITH PORK AND SHRIMPS

$\frac{3}{4}$ lb. skinless fins
$\frac{1}{2}$ lb. pork
$\frac{1}{4}$ lb. shrimps
$\frac{1}{2}$ cabbage
4 slices bamboo shoots
6 mushrooms
6 tbsp. soya sauce
6 tbsp. sherry
1 cupful brown pork gravy
2 tbsp. cornflour
1 tsp. sugar
Salt
4 lbs. lard

Cut the cabbage into $1\frac{1}{2}$ in. square pieces. Fry together with mushrooms for three minutes. Remove from heat.

Fry the bampoo shoots, which have been cut into $\frac{1}{6}$ in. thick slices across the grain, for three minutes with a little salt. Remove from pan.

Shell the shrimps and cut the pork into ribbons. Cook shrimps by boiling in a cupful of water with a little salt for two minutes. Drain. Fry them with pork for four minutes over fierce heat. Add sherry, soya sauce and cut cabbage. Stir for five minutes and transfer the contents of the frying-pan to a saucepan. Add one cup of brown pork gravy, and one cup of chicken broth. Simmer for ten minutes.

Now add the softened fins and continue to boil for five minutes. Thicken with half a cupful of a mixture of water, cornflour and sugar. When the saucepan boils again pour the contents into a deep dish. Garnish by placing the ham, bamboo shoots and shrimps on top of the fins.

Both of the shark's fin dishes are regarded as delicacies and are served only at banquets.

5. FRIED FROGS WITH CHESTNUTS

3 fat frogs
6 oz. chestnuts
6 mushrooms
1 tsp. chopped ginger
2 tsp. soya sauce
3 tsp. sherry
1 spring onion
2 tbsp. lard
½ tsp. salt

Skin the frogs and chop each one into six to eight pieces. Soak the chestnuts in hot water for half an hour. Skin and dry.

Fry the frogs in lard with chestnuts and salt for two minutes over a high heat. Add mushrooms and chopped onions, and all the seasonings, and fry for a further three minutes, stirring continually over a high heat.

6. VELVETEEN OF PORK

> 2 lb. lean pork
> 2 tbsp. sherry
> 4 tbsp. soya sauce
> 1 cup chicken broth
> 1 tbsp. fermented soya paste
> ½ tbsp. sugar
> ½ tsp. salt
> 3 tbsp. peanut oil

Cut the pork into ½ in. squares. Boil in chicken broth for one and a half hours over a very low heat, until thoroughly cooked. Remove from pan and drain, if any broth is left at all. Now place the pork in a heavy pot or deep frying-pan, in which the peanut oil has been heated to boiling. Add all the seasonings, and continue the frying over a fierce heat for five minutes, stirring vigorously all the time. Now lower the fire and insert an asbestos mat under the pan, and carry on with the frying, but continue to stir all the time, to prevent any sticking to the bottom of the pan. Continue until the colour of the meat has become rich brown, and the meat itself has become completely dried (this would take about forty minutes). In order to complete the process of dehydration and disintegration of the meat fibre, continue over a minimum fire for fifteen more minutes. When ready the pork should be in a velvety state, dark reddish brown in colour and almost melts on introduction to the mouth.

The Velveteen of Pork is more popular than the Velveteen of Beef, as it is very much smoother and more "melting". It can be fried with almost any vegetable (such as shredded cabbage, pea sprouts, etc.) simply by adding 1 tbsp. pork velveteen one and a half minutes before serving and mixing vigorously. It lends a glorious flavour to the vegetables. Since it can be preserved simply by keeping it in a jar, it is extremely useful to any housewife, quite apart from the fact that it is a great favourite in China at breakfast and for late supper. In the West, spread on a small piece of buttered toast it makes a delectable appetiser at any party.

Chapter Twelve

SNACKS AND DESSERTS

We Chinese are mainly savoury eaters as compared with Europeans, whose inclination to sweets and desserts and comparative obliviousness to the subtle blendings of savoury flavours often baffles us. Although we consume quite a large range of snacks, mostly savouries, in sweets and desserts, our numbers of recipes are comparatively limited as measured against the Western counterparts. The following are a few of the most popular snacks and desserts consumed in China.

1. PAO-TZU OR STUFFED STEAMED BUN

3 cups flour   ½ cake of yeast
½ lb. minced pork
1½ tbsp. soya sauce
½ tbsp. sesame oil (or salad oil)
1 tsp. salt
1 tsp. sugar
1 spring onion

(*a*) Savoury Pao-tzu.
Prepare the dough by first of all dissolving half a cake of yeast in one cup of warm water. This water is mixed with the flour to knead into a dough, which is put into a basin and placed in a comparatively warm place to give it time for the dough to rise. After about three to four hours the dough will have risen about three to four times its original

size. Now take the dough out and, using a quantity of flour as dusting powder, work each portion (divide dough first into a dozen portions) by rolling into flat round shapes (about ¼ in. thick and 3 in. dia.).

Meanwhile, mix the minced pork with chopped onion and seasonings and work it into a stuffing. Take a piece of flat round dough in your left hand and place about one to two tablespoonsful of this stuffing in the centre of the dough. With your right fingers turn up the sides of the dough to wrap around the stuffings until only a small opening is left at the top. This opening is finally closed by pinching the edges together.

Now place all these uncooked buns or dumplings in a hot steamer and steam for fifteen to twenty minutes. These stuffed steamed buns are served at tea-time in China.

(b) Sweet Pao-tzu.

The sweet stuffing for, say, twelve pieces of sweet Pao-tzu should consist of ½ cup of almonds, ½ cup of walnuts, ½ cup of sesame seeds, 4 tbsp. sugar, 2 tbsp. honey, 1 tbsp. lard. Grind the nuts and mix thoroughly with the remainder of the ingredients. Use this as the stuffing and proceed exactly as for the previous recipe.

(c) Pao-tzu stuffed with crab meat.

Use the meat of two large crabs (instead of pork) which have previously been cooked by steaming. Apart from the other ingredients from which the stuffing is made add ½ tsp. ground ginger and two extra onions.

(d) Vegetarian Pao-tzu.

Spinach and leek are frequently used as stuffings. About 1½ lb. of vegetables would be required. The vegetable is first minced and mixed with the seasonings. The addition of one piece of chopped pickled vegetable and an extra 1 tsp. of sesame oil would strengthen the flavour.

It is often interesting or amusing to prepare vegetarian, meat-stuffed, crab-stuffed and sweet-stuffed Pao-tzu at the same time, and steam them all together in the same steamer, but give each type a marking outside to distinguish it from the others.

2. CHIAO-TZU, OR STUFFED DUMPLINGS

This is another of our preparations which is capable of a large variety of stuffings, but in this case the stuffings are mainly of meat.

The main difference between this recipe and the previous one is that the wrapping dough is made into a thin skin without the addition of yeast. This dough is prepared by mixing two cups of flour with ½ tsp. of salt, and sufficient water to make into a very light dough. This is kneaded and rolled into a long strip about 1 in. in diameter. Cut away about 1 in. of it at a time to roll and press into round flat skin-thick cakes, circular in shape and 3 in. in diameter.

In preparing the stuffing for wrapping in the dough, use the same ingredients as in the previous recipe, but cabbage and bamboo shoots are sometimes added into the mixture. Only about ½ tbsp. of stuffing mixtures are used at a time to be wrapped in each piece of circular skin-like dough. The dough is wrapped around the stuffing in a half-moon shape and the edges are pinched or pressed together. Generally several dozen pieces of these dumplings are made at a time. They can be placed in a steamer to steam for ten minutes or they can be boiled for the same length of time. When served, they are generally dipped in vinegar and soya sauce before eating.

3. SPRING ROLLS

Spring rolls are so called because they are eaten in the spring, or soon after the Old Chinese New Year, which generally falls in February. The main feature of the spring roll is that it is a stuffed roll (meat and chopped vegetable stuffing wrapped in envelope fashion) fried in deep fat. The same stuffing as in the previous recipe can be used, but half the contents as a rule consist of pea sprouts. The dough skin for wrapping the stuffing is made as follows and requires considerable skill:

Make a mixture of $\frac{1}{4}$ lb. flour with one cup of water. Heat a small frying-pan over a low even heat. Grease the pan evenly with fat. Wipe it over with a grease-soaked cloth. Now pour a tablespoonful of the thin dough mixture in the centre of the pan. Let it run evenly over the flat bottom of the pan. Leave it there until quite dry. Turn it over a plate and peel it off. Repeat until you have sufficient number of skins for your purpose.

In making the spring rolls place about 2 tbsp. of the stuffing across the centre of the skin, about $2\frac{1}{2}$ in. long. Fold up both ends of the dough first and then the sides. Finally close the edges with a little water. When you have made sufficient number of rolls fry them in deep fat for about four minutes, immediately before serving. It is, as a rule, necessary to fry the stuffing up to two to three minutes before rolling it in the dough to ensure that it will be quite cooked after the final frying, which should render the outside of the roll quite crispy. This is an easily acceptable dish to those people of these islands who are fond of deep-fried food, such as fish and chips, etc.

4. FRIED SWEET POTATO

1 lb. sweet potato
4 tbsp. peanut oil
½ cup syrup

Steam the syrup in a bowl in a large panful of water for ten to twelve minutes. Cut the potato, which is often ½ ft. long by 3–4 in. in diameter, into thin slices of ½ in. width by 2–3 in. length. Fry them in oil for three to four minutes until they are beautifully golden brown. Remove from heat and arrange them on a hot plate. Pour the hot syrup over them and serve.

5. ALMOND TEA

2 cups blanched almonds
4 tbsp. rice
2 tbsp. sugar.

Grind the almond and rice in a mortar until they have become a very fine powder. Place this in a basin and add five cups of water. Stir and leave to stand for one and a half hours. Strain through a cheese-cloth. Add a cupful of milk. Simmer in a double boiler for two hours, stirring now and then. Now add sugar, and a pinch of salt. Bring to boil once more before serving.

Almond tea can also be served in the form of a jelly, by dissolving in it 1 tbsp. of gelatine, and placing the mixture in a refrigerator for a couple of hours.

Chapter Thirteen

CHINA TEA

There is no doubt that the Chinese and British are the greatest tea-drinkers in the world. It is quite possible (though not undebatable) that the British, per head, drink more tea than anybody else in the world, not excluding even the Chinese. If this is true, the British must have overtaken the Chinese in tea drinking in comparatively recent years of energetic and welfare state operation. For it was not more than a hundred and fifty years ago, that tea was still extremely expensive, whilst in China tea has been a popular drink for nearly a thousand years.

Although the colloquial British word "cha" and the Chinese character "Tcha" which are phonetically synonymous, are probably the one common denominator between the two entirely different languages, the way in which we regard and imbibe this beverage is quite different. To the British it is a warming and strengthening drink. It first of all warms and wakes you up at breakfast. It helps to carry you on through the long morning, during elevenses. Although it is an important aid to social intercourse at tea-time in the afternoon, to the vast majority of working people it is an all-important pick-me-up and strengthening agent to reinforce you against the wear and tear and the drag of the day. If you have high tea instead of dinner in the evening, tea acts as an agent to warm you up and prepare you for all the comforts of home and hearth.

But to the Chinese tea is essentially a refreshing drink.

It is drunk after every meal. For continual household or office use it is made in a pot which is placed inside a padded upholstered basketwork to keep warm, and used every few minutes throughout the day, much as the cigarette is resorted to in this country. When entertaining guests tea is not made in a pot, but in individual lidded cups. These cups open wide upwards and the lids sit inside the cup. When the tea is made the water in the cup floats just above the edge of the lid, which enables it to be sipped easily by the tea-drinker. The lid, which helps to keep all the tea-leaves unseen under cover, is as a rule only opened when more boiling water is required to be added or when the drinker wishes to smell the aroma of the brewing tea. The polite visitor would therefore lift the three-piece affair (cup, lid and saucer) up to his mouth with both his hands, and sip his tea (here considerable sipping noise is permissible) while he converses with his host. As each cup of tea is made independently, with its own portion of tea and dried flower, quite a lot of tea has to be used for each round of guests, irrespective of the time of day of their arrival, since a cup of tea is always the first thing to be presented as soon as the visitor crosses the threshold, whether morning, noon or night.

Not such a long time ago, tea was, practically speaking, the only universal beverage for quenching thirst in China through her annual long hot summers. To meet the demands of the hundreds of millions of thirsty mouths the quantity consumed per annum must be colossal. It is doubtful whether any reliable statistics are available which would make it possible for a fair comparison to be made with the quantity consumed in this country, where a cup of "cha" is one of the first essentials in life to cushion or bolster up the human spirit.

Since tea is a refreshing rather than a strengthening agent in China, it is drunk pure. Never is it allowed to be polluted with milk, or made heavy and syrupy with a load of sugar, although sometimes one single piece of rock-sugar is added to give it a touch of sweetness. On the other hand the blending of the various forms of tea with various forms of fresh and dried flowers to give it the traditional fragrance is a matter of such tradition and art that one has to have the discriminating palate of a wine-taster, plus the sensitive nostrils of a perfume expert, to be a connoisseur.

Among the legions of blends of tea in China, "The Fragrant Petal" is one of the most popular and best known. Often the fragrance is provided by putting fresh jasmine buds in the tea during the packing. In Foochow, where I was born and partly bred, and which during the second half of the nineteenth century was one of the greatest tea-towns in the world, jasmine are grown in profusion in the spring. The girl tea pickers and packers wear jasmines in the hair and behind their ears as they work.

Other flowers which are often used to add fragrance to tea are roses and chrysanthemums. Among the other better-known brands of tea are "The Dragon Well" blend, a green and slightly bitter variety from Chekiang, "The Iron Goddess of Mercy" from Fukien, which are drunk only in small quantities like a liqueur, "The Black Dragon" brand from Kwangtung, which is a red tea; and the "Misty Cloud" blend from Kiangsi. There are many other popular blends from Central and South West China, which to Europeans verges on the medicinal herbs, the brews from which are too unusual for daily indulgence, but are useful for either their tonic or healing qualities. There is no doubt that some of them are far more effective than aspirin for curing colds and 'flu, if you are prepared to imbibe a pint.

The attitude of a Chinese tea connoisseur towards a cup of tea is, in fact, very similar to that of an Englishman towards a globular glass of brandy; they both hold their containers with both their hands and raise them to their heads not without a slight stir of emotional satisfaction. The Englishman takes a sniff at the brandy by pushing his nose into the glass; the Chinese takes his sniff by slightly tipping the lid of his cup. As they sniff and sip, the hole in both their pockets becomes bigger and bigger. It is not unknown in China for a man to go bankrupt through drinking tea.

Chapter Fourteen

SELECTION OF DISHES

A. MENU FOR TWO PERSONS

(*a*) Pork pellet and watercress soup (p. 40).
(*b*) Steamed egg with minced meat (p. 95).
(*c*) Fried pork ribbons with young leeks (p. 55).
(*d*) Fried lettuce (p. 79).

B. MENU FOR THREE PERSONS

Add any one of the following dishes to the previous menu:

(*a*) Sliced fish in sweet and sour sauce (p. 87).
(*b*) Prawns fried in shells (p. 89).
(*c*) Deep fried fish (in pieces) (p. 86).

C. MENU FOR FOUR TO SIX PERSONS

Add one of the following soups, and one of the following meat dishes to menu for three:

(*a*) Meatball and transparent noodle soup (p. 41).
(*b*) Ham and spring green soup (p. 47).
(*c*) Beef and turnip soup (p. 48).
(*d*) "Tung-Po" or Chinese casserole of Pork (p. 52).
(*e*) Sliced beef fried with tomatoes (p. 62).
(*f*) Stewed mutton with turnips (p. 64).

D. MENU FOR SIX TO TEN PERSONS

Add two of the following dishes to the menu for four to six persons:

(a) White cut chicken (p. 68).

(b) Diced chicken meat fried with walnut (p. 89).

(c) Egg omelet with assorted ingredients (p. 94).

(d) Ham and egg dumplings (p. 97).

(e) Fried beef ribbons with onions (p. 61).

(f) Fried kidney with spring onions and cauliflower (p. 60).

A. A NORTH CHINA MENU. (Eaten with Man-tou or steamed dough dumpling).

(a) Roast duck (Peking style).

(b) Cream savoury cabbage.

(c) Prawns fried in shells.

(d) Fried thick-sliced mutton with leeks.

(e) Meat-ball and Chinese transparent (pea-starch) noodle soup.

(f) Fried sliced pork Fu-yung (egg white).

(g) Deep-fried "eight-piece" spring chicken.

B. A SOUTH CHINA MENU. (Eaten with rice).

(a) Fish ball soup (Fukien).

(b) Fried beef in oyster sauce (Canton).

(c) Steamed pork with salted fish.

(d) Deep-fried paper-wrapped chicken.

(e) Fried spinach.

(f) Plain fried Chinese sausage (Lap Chung).

(g) Fried sliced awabi with bamboo shoots.

(h) Sliced fish steamed with bean curd.

C. AN EAST CHINA MENU. (Eaten with rice).

(*a*) Smoked chicken (in pieces).

(*b*) Bamboo shoots fried with pork ribbons.

(*c*) Drunken crab (raw crab soaked in wine, sugar, etc.).

(*d*) Braised pork in pieces, or Tung-po pork.

(*e*) Mushroom and chicken soup.

(*f*) Steamed clams.

(*g*) Fried mushrooms and bean curd.

D. A WEST-CENTRAL CHINA MENU. (Eaten with rice).

(*a*) Diced chicken fried with pimento.

(*b*) Rice-powdered steamed pork.

(*c*) Pork ribbons fried with pickled vegetables (Tsa Tsai).

(*d*) Fried sweet and sour spare ribs with chopped chilli.

(*e*) Fried shelled prawns with pea sprouts.

(*f*) Fried Pumpkin (cut in pieces).

(*g*) Pig's trotter soup.

(*h*) Egg-meat dumpling and sauce.

E. AN ALL-CHINA MENU. (No rice served).

(1) Chinese meat dumplings (or Chiao-tzu).

(2) Bird's (Sea Swallow) nest and minced chicken soup.

(3) Sweet and sour spare ribs.

(4) Steamed chicken in soup.

(5) Lobsters with eggs in meat sauce.

(6) Prawns fried with green peas.
(7) Stewed mutton with orange peel.
(8) Braised leg of pork.
(9) Fried kidney with bamboo shoot.
(10) Mushroom and bean curd soup.
(11) Creamed bamboo shoot.
(12) Shark's fins with crabs.
(13) Braised carp with stuffing.
(14) Eight-treasure rice.
(15) Almond tea.

INDEX

NOTES